Contents

Receiving Love
Workbook

Receiving Love
Workbook

A Unique Twelve-Week Course
for Couples and Singles

Harville Hendrix, Ph.D.

and

Helen LaKelly Hunt, Ph.D.

ATRIA BOOKS

NEW YORK   LONDON   TORONTO   SYDNEY

ATRIA BOOKS

1230 Avenue of the Americas
New York, NY 10020

ISBN-13: 978-0-7434-8371-1
ISBN-10:   0-7434-8371-5

First Atria Books trade paperback edition April 2006

Design by Nancy Singer Olaguera/ISPN

10 9 8 7 6 5 4 3 2 1

ATRIA BOOKS is a trademark of Simon & Schuster, Inc.

Manufactured in the United States of America

For information regarding special discounts for bulk purchases,
please contact Simon & Schuster Special Sales at 1-800-456-6798
or business@simonandschuster.com.

A Special Dedication

Jean Coppock Staeheli has been our writer and friend for many years. We want to express a special appreciation for her tireless work in bringing this project to fruition. From many random notes, conversations, and case illustrations, she has used her considerable writing talents to bring order out of chaos. We owe her a debt of gratitude for her perseverance during these months and her patience with us as we attempted to make sense out of the material. Thank you Jean.

Dedication

This book is dedicated to the Board of Imago Relationships International, Inc., a nonprofit organization created and run by Imago therapists committed to providing service to Imago therapists worldwide, and dedicated to the mission of transforming the world one couple at a time.

Receiving and Giving

I'm a novice when it comes to receiving.
Giving has become my expertise.
But giving alone without getting
Becomes soon a fatal disease.

If the intake valve is not opened
There's no way to maintain a supply.
There comes a point in the cycle of life
When the out-going stream runs dry.

Straining out love from a vacuum
Is like drinking from the heart of stone.
Try as we may, at the end of the day,
We're exhausted, frustrated, alone.

'Better to give than receive," we are taught.
Yet another truth I've learned just by living:
Only the soul with the grace to receive,
Excels in the fine art of living.

The Rev. Dr. James A. Forbes, Jr.
Senior Pastor, The Riverside Church, NYC

HOW TO USE THE *RECEIVING LOVE WORKBOOK*

If you are in a committed relationship that isn't as close or fulfilling as you want it to be, this study guide is exactly right for you. Perhaps the intimacy and excitement that were there in the beginning have gone, or perhaps they were never there at all. Things are getting worse as the years pass, not better. You find yourself thinking it might make sense to end this relationship and find a partner who loves you more and can offer you the kind of hope and security you long for.

Perhaps you're upset by the indifferent or hostile way you and your partner are connecting with each other. You often feel like you're "talking past" each other. You don't seem to care about each other's thoughts and feelings, or you become offended and defensive whenever you venture out beyond the safety of routine information. You might be able to decide who's going to pick up the dry cleaning or take the kids to practice, but anything more personal feels as if you're slipping into dangerous territory.

One wife we know described what it was like when she and her husband were living in this state of conflict: "We were nothing more than roommates—roommates who didn't even like each other." They fought over everything, and couldn't stop doing battle in front of their children. It didn't take long for their pain to begin to poison the lives of their two young sons. The younger son had nightmares, and the older was showing disturbing signs of aggression in school. This couple finally reached out for help when they realized that their relationship problems were having a serious, negative impact on their children.

Sometimes, though, relationship problems are not so visible or openly expressed. Maybe you feel disappointed with your partner, rather than angry or resentful. You're sad when you think about how seldom the two of you feel any closeness. When you think of sharing feelings of excitement or anxiety, you don't think of your partner first. You think of your mother or your best friend. You are frustrated by how difficult even the simplest interactions have become. Why is the normal give-and-take in your relationship so hard? Other people seem to be able to ask one another for help, show appreciation, and get along with good feelings most of the time. Why can't you?

The professional work we've been engaged in for the last twenty years or so has been an attempt to answer this question. What makes some relationships turn into fulfilling partnerships, and others into minefields of resentment and mistrust? How can the minefield evolve into a safe ground for nurturing growth? How can you turn your committed relationship into a partnership that heals your past wounds and fosters your wholeness?

The *Receiving Love Workbook* is a twelve-week course designed to help you and your partner work through the exercises in Part III of *Receiving Love*. This guide provides you with the complete step-by-step instructions and examples you would get if you participated in a Couples' Workshop or worked with an Imago Relationship Therapist. *Each of you should have your own copy of this workbook so you can each answer questions in your own book, with the privacy you want and need.*

The purpose of the *Receiving Love Workbook* is to help you explore the consequences that self-rejection has had in your individual lives and in your relationship as a couple. One of the most significant and universal consequences of self-rejection is that it leads to an inability to receive love. Once you have an understanding of how self-rejection has kept you from being nourished by the love, appreciation, and support of those close to you, you are ready to take specific steps to surmount the self-rejection and heal its causes.

The most exciting truth we've discovered is that it's possible for problematic relationships to become sources of healing and strength. Yes, you can bring back marriages that are on the brink of divorce. The same relationship that is now causing you grief can become the source of your personal happiness and spiritual growth.

At every life stage and in every way, we become who we are through our relationships. Injuries to our self-concept occur through our relationships with our parents in childhood. These injuries manifest themselves as problems in our committed adult relationships. And, these injuries can only be healed in committed adult relationships. The very person who is the "cause" of our unhappiness holds the key to our liberation from pain.

Before beginning this workbook, please read all of *Receiving Love* by Harville Hendrix, Ph.D., and Helen LaKelly Hunt, Ph.D. We also recommend that you read *Getting the Love You Want,* though it is not essential for the successful completion of these exercises. Your successful participation in the process detailed in this workbook will be greatly facilitated by having an understanding of Imago Relationship Therapy. What follows is a summary discussion of the fundamental dynamics of intimate relationships, as conceptualized in Imago. (Please refer to *Getting the Love You Want* for a more complete discussion of Imago Relationship Therapy.)

HOW IMAGO RELATIONSHIP THERAPY UNDERSTANDS RELATIONSHIPS

You are reading this workbook because your committed relationship isn't as close and loving as you would like it to be. You may feel like this is your fault, or your partner's fault, or you may blame rotten circumstances for your discontent. But before you decide that your relationship was a mistake, consider this: there are certain principles or "laws" that are operative in all relationships. These laws function independently of who you and your partner are as individuals, and what your particular circumstances are. They serve as general rules about the way we, as human beings, fall in love and form relationships over time. Like everyone else, *your* choice of a mate and the way you connect to the person you've chosen has been influenced by factors within you that you are not conscious of.

Your Choice of Partner Is No Accident
Let's start with the first reality: Your parents were not perfect. No matter how hard they tried or what good people they were, they were not undamaged enough themselves to be perfectly attuned to your unique and wonderful self. They did not support your development through the stages of childhood in just the right way that would bring out and strengthen *all* aspects of your temperament and personality.

So, the chances are good that you emerged from childhood with problems or unresolved difficulties with at least one of your parents. Glad to be finally out of your parents' house and making your own decisions, you probably fell in and out of love several times, learning something of value each time. At some point, you chose the person you hoped would be your life partner. Obviously, this person attracted you on many different levels. If asked, you could list all the reasons you fell in love.

But you wouldn't be able to list all the reasons you were attracted. None of us would. That's because we have an unconscious attraction to potential partners who offer us the chance to work out unresolved problems from our childhood. As surprising as it may seem, we are drawn to people who have some of the same traits, characteristics, attitudes, beliefs, and/or behaviors as the parent who gave us the most trouble when we were children. This attraction would *have* to be unconscious, because who would commit to someone with problematic traits on purpose?

Once we get over our amazement at this trick of the subconscious, we can see that nature has actually handed us a fabulous opportunity. As an adult, we now have the chance to understand and heal the leftover wounds we sustained as children. If you think about it, you can see that only a partner who gave you a chance to work out the problems you were already carrying could offer you the opportunity to reclaim your wholeness.

If, say, you were fortunate enough to reach adulthood at peace with your intelligence but worried about your ability to get along with people, then a partner who did not challenge you to become more adept socially might seem like a good match. But you would miss out on the chance to grow in the area in which you need to grow more socially skilled. A partner who is a perfect mirror cannot stretch you into greater wholeness. That's why we say that the purpose of committed relationships is to help you heal and become whole. It is in the course of doing the healing *work* that we find happiness.

THE COURSE OF LOVE IS WELL-ESTABLISHED

The word "work" probably alerts you to the fact that healing isn't easy. And that brings up something else you have to know: all romantic relationships go through stages. In the first stage, you don't see the echo of childhood problems your partner embodies. You only see how beautiful, intelligent, funny, loving, talented, and sexy he or she is. You are in love and the world is a glorious place. Thank heavens for this stage of bliss. It affords some time-limited protection from the harder realities of life.

The second stage, however, is a challenge. This is the Power Struggle, which is where you probably are now. The rose-colored glasses of romantic love lose their tint, and you start seeing your partner in the cold, hard light of day. The same things that bugged you about your father are now starting to get you steamed about your husband. Only this time, you're not going to cave in to another man's arrogance and bossiness. You're a grown woman and you're going to fight! Or, let's say you're a man and your wife talks at you incessantly, just as your mother used to. It feels like more than you can bear. When you were a kid, you couldn't run too far away from your mother, but you can darn sure find ways to hide from your wife.

For many couples, the Power Struggle is where they get stuck and stay stuck. It takes outside guidance and dedication by the two partners to work through this second stage and emerge into the third stage—Mature Love. Helping couples into the third stage is the purpose of our work in Imago Relationship Therapy. Mature Love is the oasis you can reside in, once you've crossed the desert of the Power Struggle. This is the stage where all the work that has gone before allows you to create a conscious relationship that is secure and lasting.

In Mature Love, you know yourself and your partner inside and out. You understand your histories. You have learned how to communicate, how to negotiate differences, and how to honor your individuality while strengthening your attachment. Completing the exercises in this workbook will be a significant contribution toward helping you reach the oasis of Mature Love.

One could say that this workbook is primarily for couples who are in the Power Struggle, who are trying to understand each other better and find a way to live peacefully. But because the central focus in this workbook is on how hard it is to let down barriers and receive love, we are addressing a subject that is larger than the stressful interactions that are part of the Power Struggle.

In fact, the following twelve sessions and their exercises are suitable for *anyone* who is unable or reluctant to let appreciation and support into their hearts and bodies, as well as their minds. Anyone in any situation can come to the realization that they can't accept compliments, have trouble accepting help, and turn aside protestations of love. For that reason, you can benefit from using this workbook, whether you are madly in love, a disgruntled or reluctant partner, or someone enjoying the fruits of many years of relationship building.

The sessions are constructed to help you understand why you have the beliefs and behaviors you do, where they came from in your childhood, how your behavior fits with your partner's, and how the changes you desire in your relationship can only occur when the two of you work together to achieve them. The goal is to help you become a more receptive partner, someone who can be nourished by the gifts of love that are everywhere around you.

UNDERSTANDING THE DEFENSES OF MAXIMIZING AND MINIMIZING

One of the goals of this workbook is to help you identify the behaviors you use when you feel threatened emotionally. Everybody has defenses. Usually, they are so ingrained that we're hardly aware of what our defenses are—although it's a safe bet that our partners would be able to tell us. One's defensive behavior tends to be obvious to other people.

An important concept in Imago Relationship Therapy involves maximizing and minimizing behaviors. We thought it would be helpful to discuss this concept here, so you will be familiar with these terms when you encounter them in the exercises. You will especially need to know what they mean as you complete Session 10.

Childhood wounds lead to the development of either maximizing or minimizing tendencies in adulthood, and partners who maximize and partners who minimize tend to pair with each other. Maximizers tend to exaggerate their energy, escalate their feelings, express intense emotions, and confuse their feelings with facts. When you ask maximizers what they think, they will tell you what they feel. Minimizers tend to diminish their energy by holding on to their feelings and showing little emotion. They are mainly interested in facts rather than feelings. When you ask minimizers what they feel, they will tell you what they think. Both maximizing and minimizing are survival tactics that have become habitual.

Everyone has elements of both maximizing and minimizing within them, since holding energy in and expressing energy outward are natural forms of defense. In early life, either maximizing or minimizing becomes dominant and habitual because it is effective in creating a feeling of safety. The imbalance, however, is ineffective in adult intimate partnerships because it creates danger, and thus fear, in the other partner. This results in a rupture of connection.

To clarify this concept further, let's look at an example based on the couple used as an illustration in Session 9. Sally and Jim were amazed to find how well their wounds fit together. Sally had rebelled against the social straitjacket she thought her parents had tried to keep her in. Her way of fighting for her individuality was to withdraw her attention and her affection. This is something she did with Jim whenever she started boiling inside at his constant checking and double-checking of whatever she was doing.

Jim was stung by his wife's withdrawals. Whenever she got quiet and uncommunicative, he compensated by becoming more expressive and emotional. He had the fear that Sally might not like him if he was too adamant about his own concerns and opinions, so he coped with her silence by becoming overly solicitous about what she wanted and how she was feeling.

Sally and Jim came to understand that the most effective way partners can facilitate healing for each other is to become more like the other, especially, more like the part that they dislike in the partner. This means that maximizers need to contain their energy by minimizing more, and minimizers need to express their energy by maximizing more. It is a core change, one that is difficult and often takes a long time depending upon the depth of the wound and the rigidity of the defense. However, it is the greatest opportunity we have to promote healing in our intimate relationships.

A NOTE TO THOSE WHO ARE SINGLE

It's true that our work is focused on relationships—their fundamental importance, what makes them work, and how people can make them better. But, you can get a lot out of this workbook if you happen to be single. You can sharpen your ability to recognize, validate, and act on your desires. You can discover which messages your caretakers instilled in you when you were young. You can identify your own hidden prohibitions against giving and receiving. You can discover your strengths as giver and receiver, and clarify which areas you would like to improve. You can learn how to engage in Imago Dialogue and use these techniques for all of your important communications, whether you have a partner or not. And, you can construct a growth plan to help you move past self-rejection and reclaim those parts of yourself that have been lost through neglect or disapproval.

We are explicit about our belief that the work of self-acceptance is best accomplished with a partner. But, much can be accomplished alone. And most of the journey can be accomplished with a friend who is willing to participate with you in this adventure of self-discovery. You will notice that many of the instructions remind you that you can complete this exercise with a friend if you don't have a partner.

THE PROBLEM WITH NOT BEING ABLE
TO RECEIVE LOVE

The suggested reading at the beginning of each session will give you the theoretical background you need to complete the exercises. But we will briefly summarize here why difficulty receiving love is a problem, where the problem comes from, and how it can be overcome.

Barriers to receiving love are so common that we often don't recognize them. When someone dismisses a compliment or minimizes an accomplishment, we are more likely to praise them for being modest than to recognize that we've just witnessed a symptom of self-hatred. Most people don't make the connection. How does self-hatred, or self-rejection as we prefer to call it, lead to an inability to accept the physical, psychological, and spiritual gifts that love offers?

Inevitably as children, some aspects of our whole selves are supported and encouraged, and some are not. Because our one and only imperative as children is to stay safe, to stay alive, we will chop off parts of our real selves and add on parts to our false selves in order to stay in our caretakers' good graces. To be banished, emotionally or otherwise, is tantamount to death. We would rather distort our true beings than be rejected.

This process of making up a socially acceptable public persona while starving out some of our legitimate desires, impulses, traits, and talents goes on without our being aware of it. First, it happens when we're only children. Second, like other crucial psychological processes, this one is largely unconscious. What that means is that by the time we are adults, we are torn and jagged. The wholeness we were born with has been eaten away to a greater or lesser degree, and a whole section of ourselves is lost to our own awareness. These lost parts are what cause our problems with receiving.

Simply put, we can't accept acknowledgment or praise or nurturing for the parts of us we don't recognize in ourselves. Other people may see our lost parts without any trouble. But because our connection to these aspects of ourselves has been severed, we don't get it when someone compliments them. We don't even recognize that we have these traits, or we know only that they have been the source of psychic pain. We are thus unable to hug this gift to our hearts and be warmed by its glow.

The effect of this self-rejection and our consequent inability to receive love can be quite serious for our relationships. Initially, it may be annoying to a husband that his wife can't allow him to give her a compliment. But, eventually, the husband may lose heart and start to question his ability to have a positive influence on his wife. This is sad for both of them. But, at the other end of the spectrum, a partner who believes he is no good can destroy not only himself, but his wife, and even worse, his children. And that is tragic.

This kind of private tragedy easily becomes part of the social cost; we all pay for addiction, infidelity, divorce, abuse, crime, disrupted schools, and mental illness or dysfunction. A person with significant portions of himself or herself disowned or unrecognized has trouble forming successful relationships, and is unable to take in the positive feedback and actual help that would begin to restore his or her lost self, and by extension, our social ills.

The solution to this problem is two-fold: (1) learn more about your childhood wounds and how they have led to your pattern of self-rejection and resistance to receiving love, and (2) reclaim these lost parts of yourself by learning to love those parts in your partner. This last task is a little tricky. Since your partner manifests (some of) the parts of you that you have disowned, when you love them in your partner, you are, in effect, loving them in yourself. "Loving" here means recognizing and forming a positive relationship with those traits you have heretofore refused to acknowledge or have acknowledged only in a disparaging way.

Here's an example. Karen's natural desire to explore new experiences on her own as a child was not supported by her overprotective mother. When Karen married Karl, she was aware of being uncomfortable with some of the more adventurous decisions Karl made about how to spend his free time. This conflict came to a head when Karl sold his business and bought a 35-foot sailboat with his extra cash. His vision was that he and Karen and their son would take the boat out overnight and sail up and down the coast.

Karen wanted to enjoy being on the water, but she freaked out any time Karl took the boat out, either with friends or alone together. It just felt too dangerous. Through reading *Receiving Love* and using this workbook, she learned that a good way to begin to reclaim her lost self (that is, her capacity for exploring) would be for her to accept and preferably, encourage, her husband's efforts to involve her in his sailing adventures. This was hard for Karen and frustrating for Karl, who simply wanted to go sailing, but he was patient and she was courageous, and they finally got to the point where they could go out and enjoy being on the water together.

HOW THE *RECEIVING LOVE WORKBOOK* WILL HELP YOU GIVE AND RECEIVE THE LOVE YOU WANT

WHAT YOU WILL ACCOMPLISH

In the exercises you and your partner complete together in this workbook, you will:

1. Recognize the gifts you are being given and learn to give gifts to your partner.
2. Learn a way of communicating through Imago Dialogue that will change your relationship for the better.
3. Figure out whether you are a separate or connected knower, and discover how your mode of knowing intersects with your partner's, and what implication this has for your relationship.
4. Practice giving and receiving with your partner.
5. Experience what it's like to flood your partner with positive appreciation and receive the same from your partner.
6. Examine the attitudes and behaviors that characterize how you receive.
7. Examine the attitudes and behaviors that characterize how you give.
8. Learn how childhood messages and messages from your partner have influenced your ability to give and receive.
9. Understand more completely how and why you have the defensive patterns you use in your relationship.
10. Identify your childhood wound and learn how it has affected your relationship.
11. Reclaim your lost self.
12. Create a plan for becoming whole and increasing your ability to receive love.

Although you are responsible for doing your individual work yourself, built into the twelve sessions are opportunities at every stage to tell your partner what you have discovered and to dialogue about how both of you can make changes that will establish an easy, natural pattern of giving and receiving. If you do not have a partner, a good and willing friend makes a good partner.

THE COMMITMENT YOU ARE MAKING

In order for the process outlined in this workbook to be successful, you and your partner must commit to:

1. Completing all twelve sessions and participating actively and openly in this process to the best of your ability.
2. Completing all Between-Session Assignments.
3. Establishing safety in your relationship by creating a hospitable climate of willingness and openness in order to learn about the hidden parts of your partner and make changes that are mutually beneficial.
4. Using Imago Dialogue for sharing insights, feelings, and thoughts that arise during the course of completing the exercises in this workbook.
5. Working toward ending self-hatred in yourself and your partner. Changing the attitudes and behaviors that keep you from receiving the love your partner has to give.
6. Accepting and loving yourself and your partner.

By undertaking this commitment, you are saying to yourself and your partner that you are ready to break free from the unconscious factors that have held you prisoner to your lost self, and the self-rejection that has resulted. You are ready to learn a new way of relating where you and your partner become each other's best chance for healing and happiness.

GETTING STARTED

ORGANIZATION
The workbook is organized into twelve sessions. Each session includes the following sections:

- **Review in *Receiving Love* and/or *Getting the Love You Want*:** Material to read before the session.
- **Time Frame:** An approximate time frame for each exercise and the session as a whole. Be sure to allow more time rather than less.
- **Special Considerations:** Information to help you orient yourself toward the session.

- **What You Need to Know:** An essay that summarizes the theory behind each session and the rationale behind the exercises.
- **Exercise:** Specific step-by-step instructions and work pages for completing the exercises and discussing them with your partner. All exercises begin with a stated objective.
- **Between-Session Assignments:** Tasks to help you integrate the knowledge and new skills into your daily life.

Although we strongly recommend that you and your partner each have your own copy of this workbook, there are additional worksheets in the Appendix. These worksheets can also be used for making first drafts of your answers, or they can be used to record your responses in the future as you learn and grow from the process described in this workbook.

Do No More Than One Session Each Week

The most important consideration is that you and your partner find a way to use the workbook that maintains your commitment to the process. Some of the sessions are more complex than others, and you may find that you want to spend more than one session a week on a particular session. That's fine. But we don't recommend that you rush by trying to complete more than one session a week. Neither is it a good idea to skip a week, since you want to do what you can to maintain your momentum.

Between-Session Assignments

One day every week, you will be completing the assignments for that week's new session. On the other six days of each week, you can practice what you just learned in that week's session, *and* review material from previous sessions. Practicing and reviewing are a central part of the learning process. Between-Session Assignments will give you suggestions for how to do this.

The Between-Session Assignments may involve rereading your responses to questions to keep the material fresh in your mind, continuing to think about your responses, and adding to what you originally wrote, building on the basic ideas of the session by broadening their applicability, and most important, engaging in Imago Dialogue. You cannot practice Imago Dialogue too often. Every time you engage in the dialogue process, you are strengthening your communication skills, and you are sharing thoughts and feelings with your partner on a deep level.

It is also a good idea to refresh material you learned in previous sessions.

Which previous sessions you end up reviewing or expanding will depend on which problems are most urgent and/or where you need the most work. You will find suggestions for continuing the momentum of previous sessions in the Between-Session Assignments.

COMPLETE EACH SESSION IN ORDER AND EXACTLY AS DESCRIBED

The sessions and their exercises are sequential and build upon one another, following the principle of graduated change. The learning in one session or exercise is a prerequisite for the learning in the next. Some of the exercises are easier than others, but keep in mind that the more difficult an exercise is, the more potential it contains for growth.

SET ASIDE APPROXIMATELY TWO HOURS EACH WEEK

You will discover that doing the exercises in this workbook requires a significant amount of time and commitment. You may find that it works best for you and your partner to set aside the same time every week for completing the sessions, or it may be best for you to make a new appointment every week. Choose the arrangement that best supports your commitment to the process.

Do whatever you can to make your sessions together a welcome opportunity to move toward your goal of creating a conscious relationship. Some of the work is difficult, some of it is emotionally charged, and some of it is fun. But all of it is life-changing. Approach your participation in these sessions with energy, and respect the effort you will be making to reset old habits into new, life-giving patterns of behavior.

The introductory material for each session gives approximate times for completion. Basic guidelines are to allow more time than you think you'll need, be sure you and your partner are rested, and do what you can to ensure that you will not be distracted or interrupted.

HAVE THE FOLLOWING ITEMS AVAILABLE AT EACH SESSION

- Two copies of the *Receiving Love Workbook.*
- Two small notebooks for Session #1, and scrap paper for making notes if you wish.
- Pens or pencils.
- A clock or watch.
- Tissues and water.

HOW TO PROCEED

BEFORE BEGINNING SESSION 1:
1. Read all of *Receiving Love.*
2. Read all of "How to Use the *Receiving Love Workbook.*"
3. Review this workbook by reading the Contents or quickly scanning the whole workbook.

BEFORE EACH SESSION:
Read the suggested sections of *Receiving Love* and *Getting the Love You Want.*

DURING EACH SESSION:
1. Note the time required and any special considerations.
2. Read What You Need to Know and Objectives sections.
3. Follow step-by-step instructions for doing the exercises and discussing them with your partner.
4. Share your experiences of completing the session with your partner.
5. Make an appointment for the next session.

BETWEEN EACH SESSION:
1. Complete Between-Session Assignments.
2. Take every opportunity to be conscious of what you have just learned and to practice the new behavior you wish to become part of your relationship.

This workbook is designed to be completed over the course of three months. The amount of time needed to change a belief, modify an attitude, or stop engaging in one behavior while developing a new one can never be known for sure. It depends on the person and what he or she is trying to achieve. Since we are talking about changing a *relationship,* it really depends on *two* people and what they are trying to achieve. The one thing we can tell you with certainty, though, is that you don't change just by answering questions and filling out forms. Change requires conscious intention and effort, a commitment to practice the new behaviors, and dialogue with your partner so both of you can get feedback about your progress. The process can be summarized this way:

- *Discontent* about what isn't working.
- *Information* and guidance about how to change.
- *Commitment* to change.
- *Practice* of the desired behavior.
- Periodic *evaluation* of how you're doing.
- *Celebration* of your successes.

You are about to begin an adventure in emotional and spiritual healing. You have a committed partner. Grab every moment and every opportunity to create the relationship of your dreams!

SESSION I

The Gift Diary

REVIEW IN *RECEIVING LOVE*

    Introduction, "Learning to Know More Completely," pages 8–12

    Chapter 1, Introductory Section, pages 17–18

    Chapter 2, "An Expanded Idea of Relationship," pages 32–37

    Chapter 5, "Rejecting Love in Committed Relationships,"
        pages 106–119

    Chapter 8, "Separate and Connected Knowing," pages 174–177

    Chapter 9, "Practice Being Receptive," pages 181–182

TIME FRAME
Approximately 1 hour for setup; 10 minutes a day ongoing.

SPECIAL CONSIDERATIONS
We suggest that you and your partner each buy a small notebook that can be divided into three sections for this session. Label your notebook "My Gift Diary." Then label each section as follows: (1) "Receiving Inventory," (2) "Daily Gift Record," and (3) "Dream Gift List for My Partner."

WHAT YOU NEED TO KNOW
Most of us have been given more gifts in our lives than we are able to acknowledge. We have trouble taking in affection, praise, support, compliments, or material gifts from others. Because of past wounding, we are not always able to swallow, break down, and use this food for the soul.

    The purpose of the Gift Diary is to help you develop more awareness of the gifts you've been offered in the past and the gifts you are offered every day in the present. This session will help you to see how easy or difficult it is for you to receive them. It will also help you and your partner move away from unconscious relating toward conscious relating, by giving you the chance to acknowledge what you do for each other and what you would most like to receive from each other.

Remember that a gift is anything, tangible or intangible, that is given to you in love. Most people are offered far more gifts than they realize. Compliments, appreciations, and encouragements can glance off our hardened shells without leaving any permanent impression. The Gift Diary will help you and your partner develop an appreciation for what you have, and it will help you see where you are resistant to receiving. You have to know when you are not receptive in order to remove the barriers that are keeping you from being nourished by the love that is around you.

When you have learned the technique of the Imago Dialogue in Session 2, you can use your nightly sharing of gifts as an opportunity to practice the skills of mirroring, validating, and empathizing.

PART I: The Receiving Inventory

EXERCISE

Construct Your Receiving Inventory

Time: 45 minutes

OBJECTIVES

- To record gifts that have been given to you in the past.

- To become aware of what these gifts have meant to you.

- To receive or recall receiving these gifts.

STEP 1.

Open the first section of your diary, "Receiving Inventory." Make a list of all the gifts you've received in the past that were most valuable to you. These gifts can be from your partner, friends, coworkers, employers, past partners, family members, and so on. Your list will include material objects, expressions of support and encouragement, opportunities you were offered, signs of affection, actual help, and so on. It may help you to think about one giver at a time rather than all gifts in general. For example, write "father" and list the gifts he's given you, and then "mother" and the gifts she's given you.

EXAMPLE:

When Mary thought about her parents through the lens of what they had given her, she came up with a list that included the following:

They were not intrusive into my life.

They provided me with a range of opportunities to explore my interests.

They paid for music lessons.

They paid for my wedding.

Mary said that making this list was valuable for her because she had spent quite a bit of time in her twenties dwelling on what her parents hadn't given her. By the time she compiled her full list, which included what her siblings, friends, and husband had given her, she felt a gratitude she had never experienced before.

STEP 2.

Now, expand upon each gift you've recorded by answering the following questions. Be sure to allow enough time to explore these questions, and your answers, fully.

What did each gift mean to you?

Who gave each one to you?

How old were you when you received this gift?

What did it feel like to receive this gift?

STEP 3.

When your inventory list is complete, study each entry as an objective fact. Think rationally about what you were given, and whether or not you were able to receive each gift. Note down any important observations for each entry.

EXAMPLE:

When Mary, in the previous example, wrote about the first gift on her list—that her parents hadn't been intrusive in her life—she realized that she hadn't seen their nonintrusiveness as a gift. She had simply seen it as a fact, with negative overtones. It wasn't until she was in her midthirties and had children of her own that she could appreciate her parents' good boundaries as a gift to her.

STEP 4.

Allow yourself to move from your head to your heart, and re-create the experience of being given the gift. Whether or not you were able to receive the gift when it was first offered, let yourself receive it now. Be aware of the emotions you feel about each gift and the different levels of love you feel as you allow yourself to receive, or remember what it was like to receive in the past. Spend some time feeling connected to both the gift and the giver of the gift. Savor all the good feelings of the moment.

STEP 5.

After you and your partner have completed your inventories, share them with each other in dialogue. (See Session 2 for a complete lesson in how to use the Imago Dialogue.) Sharing in this way will allow the partner who is talking (the Sender) to absorb more completely the reality of what he or she has been given, and the one who is listening (the Receiver) will learn about the gifts that have particularly touched his or her partner.

PART II: Daily Gift Record

EXERCISE

Keep a Daily Gift Record

Time: 10 minutes

OBJECTIVES

- To open your eyes to the gifts you and your partner are trying to give each other.

- To encourage you to open your heart and notice the little things you do for each other every day.

- To expand your capacity to move from separate to connected knowing.

STEP 1.

Open the second section of your notebook, "Daily Gift Record."

It's easy for the gifts you and your partner exchange every day to get lost in your busyness and self-absorption. To guard against that, write down three gifts you receive from your partner every day. You can note little or big things.

> *EXAMPLE:*
>
> *Martin was surprised how often his wife did things to please him. He had never thought of them as gifts before. In fact, he realized that in many ways, he had taken her for granted. Here is his list for one day:*
>
> - *She watched my favorite TV program with me, even though I know she doesn't like it very much.*
> - *She cut fresh flowers and put them by my bathroom sink.*
> - *She reached out and held my hand when we walked back from the school meeting.*

STEP 2.

Before you go to bed at night, talk with your partner about the gifts you wrote down in your Daily Gift Record that day. Share with him or her what it was like for you to receive each gift, including all the sensations you experienced. This will help you grow in your capacity to receive. Tell your partner how much you appreciate his or her gifts, and share which ones had the most meaning for you. This will help your partner give to you in ways that most touch your heart.

STEP 3.

Sharing your Daily Gift Record with your partner provides an opportunity for moving from separate to connected knowing. As you share with your partner what you've written, practice opening your heart to your partner's generosity. Move into a deeper place of acceptance by saying, "I receive this as a gift. Thank you." Let yourself breathe in an awareness of the gift. Hold an image of the gift in your mind for a moment. And then, breathe out an acceptance of your partner's love. Allow yourself to feel the connection you have to your partner's gift, and ultimately, to your partner as the primary gift in your life.

STEP 4.

Sometimes, you might want to extend the gift discussion with your partner. For example, if you give gifts to your partner that he or she does not mention, ask gently whether your gesture or behavior is experienced as a gift. If your partner does experience it as a gift, you will know to keep doing it, even if your gesture is never again commented upon. If your partner responds that what you're doing doesn't seem like a gift, then you can ask what *would* seem like a gift. Show interest in your partner's feelings and thoughts about what he or she most values and appreciates. Simply being asked is a gift in itself.

EXAMPLE:

Martin was in the habit of bringing his wife the morning newspaper before she got up in the morning. There is no doubt that this was a sweet and considerate gesture, but when he asked her whether she thought of it as a gift, she confessed that she appreciated it, but she would prefer reading the paper after she took a shower. Martin was happy to know that. With a slight adjustment, he could do something for her that was right on target. And she loved being asked.

A word of caution: If your partner does not perceive what you are doing as a valuable gift, you could become resentful. If you feel that your partner is not receiving or is ungrateful, avoid blaming. Blaming makes it even more difficult for your partner to open his or her heart to receive. Take the time to ask what *would* feel like a gift to your partner, rather than becoming resentful that what *you* perceive as a valuable gift is not received in the same way by him or her.

PART III: Dream Gift List

<u>EXERCISE</u>

Keep a Dream Gift List for Your Partner

Time: 15 minutes

OBJECTIVES

- To keep a running list of what you believe your partner would like to get from you in the future.

- To increase your awareness of your partner's needs and desires.

STEP 1.

Open the last section of your diary, "Dream Gift List for My Partner."

As thoughts and ideas occur to you, create a list of things you believe your partner would like to receive from you. Use what you've learned by listening to your partner talk about the gifts he or she has received in the past (from the first exercise in this session) to get ideas for what gifts would be welcome from you.

Every so often, ask your partner to review your list for accuracy, and ask him or her to add what you haven't thought of. You, in turn, can review your partner's list and add whatever gifts *you* would like to receive. Add extra notes beside each dream gift, such as when and under what circumstances you think your partner would like to receive that gift from you. Clarify for each dream gift the following questions: What time of day, in what setting, and how often would your partner like to receive your gift? The Dream Gift List will help shift giving in your relationship from unconscious relating, based on what you *think* your partner wants, to conscious relating, based on what you now *know* your partner wants.

> *EXAMPLE:*
>
> *Margaret really wanted her husband to give her gifts that were closer to what she wanted. Every year she cringed when she opened the Weed Wacker or utility scissors or heavy-duty work gloves that were that year's Christmas present. She saw the Dream Gift List exercise as an opportunity to target her gifts to him, but also to teach him what she would love to receive.*

STEP 2.

Update your list by gathering ideas from your partner's passing comments. Here are gift ideas one husband collected from hints his wife let drop in normal conversation: a day with nothing to do, music lessons, a DVD set of Lana Turner movies, love notes left on the bathroom mirror, and a better message recorded on the phone system. By listening attentively, he was able to receive the excitement of thrilling her with things she really wanted.

It's certainly true that creating a better relationship requires work, but all work and no fun is not effective. The Dream Gift List is a way to approach the serious business of receiving and giving by adding anticipation and pleasure into the equation.

BETWEEN-SESSION ASSIGNMENTS

- Share your Daily Gift Records in Part II of this session with each other every day. Doing so will keep your awareness of the gifts that you are being offered fresh in your minds, and it will help you and your partner feel acknowledged for your efforts.
- At least once this week, add additional ideas for gifts your partner would like to receive from you to your Dream Gift List.
- At least once a month, surprise your partner with an item from the Dream Gift List.

The Imago Dialogue

REVIEW IN *RECEIVING LOVE*

> **Chapter 8,** "The Imago Dialogue," pages 162–171, and "Separate and Connected Knowing," pages 174–177
>
> **Chapter 9,** "Practice the Imago Dialogue," pages 182–183

REVIEW IN *GETTING THE LOVE YOU WANT*

> **Chapter 9,** "Increasing Your Knowledge of Yourself and Your Partner," pages 131–156

TIME FRAME

Each exercise will take approximately 30 minutes, for a total of 3 hours.

SPECIAL CONSIDERATIONS

This session may be completed in one long sitting, or it may be completed in three sittings, in which you learn how to mirror, validate, and empathize in separate steps. Agree in advance on a place and time to dialogue. You will want to be rested and free from other distractions. Let your body language show your partner that you are open and receptive to the process of hearing and experiencing his or her message to you. Remember to be nonjudgmental and nonintrusive. You want to learn what is in your partner's head and heart, so clear away your own thoughts and prepare to enter your partner's experience.

First read through this entire section. Decide who will be the Sender and who will be the Receiver. Follow the instructions for Parts I, II, and III (mirroring, validating, and empathizing). Then, in Part IV, reverse roles so the Sender becomes the Receiver, and vice versa. Finally, talk about the experience you've both had sending and receiving.

WHAT YOU NEED TO KNOW

Our work with couples emphasizes the importance of a dialogue framework that can help partners create a more conscious relationship. At its heart, dialogue delivers the core message that both of you have permission to be who you are, and to be accepted for who you are. This permission and acceptance creates safety in your relationship, and safety is a precondition for receiving love.

Three different processes make up the Imago Dialogue: mirroring, validating, and empathizing. In any given conversation, any or all of these processes might be present, though mirroring is the most fundamental and the most frequent. The Imago Dialogue is structured to ensure that you hear what the other person is saying and that you share in each other's feelings. There are specific words and phrases that move the dialogue along, but even if these words are not spoken, any interaction can still be *in the spirit* of the Imago Dialogue. When the issues between you and your partner are the most intense, the Imago Dialogue is a safe and effective way to communicate.

In addition, dialogue gives you a chance to practice the skills of accurate mirroring and logical thought, which are involved in separate knowing, and the skills of emotional resonance and empathy, which are involved in connected knowing. You are involved at the level of both the head *and* the heart. As you listen carefully to the content of what your partner is saying, you are engaging in separate knowing. Your goal is to mirror accurately what you have heard. Then, as you validate your partner's point of view, you move into connected knowing as you allow yourself to connect with your partner's reality. Finally, expressing empathy helps you achieve an even deeper level of connected knowing by opening you to your partner's feelings. The experience of empathy allows you to participate in the joy and pain of your partner by transcending the boundaries that can so easily divide the two of you. You will learn more about separate and connected knowing in Session 3.

People who are just learning the Imago Dialogue for the first time often complain that it feels like an unnatural, cumbersome way of relating. You can expect it to feel mechanical at first. But learning the steps and practicing them whenever you can will bring you great rewards. Dialogue will help you appreciate the uniqueness of each of you, while, at the same time, drawing you closer together. When dialogue is part of your relationship, you will be less reactive, feel more emotional safety, and experience a much deeper level of connection.

PART I: Mirroring

EXERCISE

Learning to Mirror

Time: 30 minutes

Mirroring is the process of accurately reflecting back the content of a message. Repeating back the content accurately is called *flat mirroring.* Flat mirroring can be more difficult than it sounds. It is very easy, without realizing it, to mirror back a little more than what was said, or a little less. A person who gives back a little more is doing *convex mirroring.* A person who gives back less, by zeroing in on one point that interests him and ignoring the rest, is doing *concave mirroring.*

Maximizers often "repeat" the message through convex mirroring by adding something of their own for the purpose, conscious or not, of shaping the other person's thoughts and feelings. (Please see Session 10 for a discussion of maximizing and minimizing.) An example of convex mirroring is the wife who mirrors back to her husband: "So you're feeling guilty that you came home late for dinner," when what the husband actually said was, "I'm sorry I didn't start for home sooner because the traffic was so bad."

Minimizers often "repeat" a message through concave mirroring by highlighting the one thing they think is important, but leaving out what the speaker thinks is most important. An example of concave mirroring is the husband who responds to his wife's difficulty with a car problem by saying, "So, you're telling me you couldn't figure out what was wrong with your car," when what his wife actually said was, "I'm delighted that I was able to get the car to the garage for repair today."

Both convex and concave mirroring are common forms of paraphrasing. When we paraphrase, we state in our own words what we think another person is saying. But we often assume that we know what the other person is saying when we really don't. We are just guessing. We may be good guessers, and we may be right most of the time, but unless we check whether we've got it right, the danger exists that we will be misunderstood. It can also be tempting during the process of mirroring to interpret before we understand fully. If our interpretation is based on errors of understanding, then our interpretation will be wrong. In contrast, besides ensuring accuracy, flat mirroring lets a partner know that you are willing to put aside your own thoughts and feelings for the moment in order to understand the other's point of view. For most people this is a rare moment of self-transcendence. It is also a moment that creates safety and deeper emotional connection in your relationship.

OBJECTIVES

- Learn to listen accurately to what your partner is saying.

- Create safety in your relationship.

- Develop clear communication and deeper emotional connection.

STEP 1.

Choose who will be the Sender and the Receiver. The Sender starts the dialogue by saying, "I would like to have an Imago Dialogue. Is now okay?" If this is not a good time, the Receiver should suggest another time as soon as possible.

STEP 2.

The Sender begins with something positive, such as an appreciation for something the Receiver has done or said. It can be as simple as, "Thank you for setting aside this time for us to talk." Then the Sender conveys what he wants to say as clearly as possible. The message should start with "I" and describe what the Sender is thinking or feeling. For this first exercise, while you are learning the technique, choose a message that is neutral. Examples of neutral subjects are: what happened at work today, how you felt about the movie you saw last night, what you want to accomplish in the next few hours, or what struck you in the magazine article you just read.

EXAMPLE:

Using Imago Dialogue, Barbara sent this message to her husband, Bill: "The weather is nice this morning. I want to get out into the yard and do some gardening."

STEP 3.

The Receiver then mirrors back what he or she has just heard the Sender say. The Receiver will find it helpful to use this sentence stem: "If I got what you just said," (and then mirror). The Receiver then checks to see whether he or she has mirrored accurately by asking, "Did I get it right?" If the Sender indicates he or she heard accurately, then the Receiver says, "Is there more you want to say about that?" If the Sender has more to say, he or she adds to the message. The Receiver continues to mirror and ask, "Is there more you want to say about that?" until the Sender has completed the message. The question, "Is there more you want to say about that?" is very important. It helps the Sender complete all of his or her thoughts and feelings, and prevents the Receiver from responding to an incomplete message. Also, since it is limited to "more about *that*," it helps the Sender limit the message to *one* subject at a time.

EXAMPLE:

*Continuing the example above, Bill mirrors what Barbara has just said: "**If I got what you just said**, you want to go out and do some gardening because the weather is nice this morning. Did I get that right?"*

> *Barbara responds: "Yes, you got it."*
> *Bill says, "**Is there more you want to say about that?**"*
> *Barbara may say "Yes" and say more, or she may say "No," finishing this part of the dialogue.*

STEP 4.

When the Sender has completed the message, the Receiver then summarizes the Sender's entire message with this sentence stem: "Let me see if I got all of that . . ." When the Receiver finishes the summary, he or she should check for accuracy with this sentence: "Did I get it all?" The summary is important because it helps the Receiver understand the Sender more deeply and to see the logic in what was said. This helps with validation, which is the next step. When the Sender acknowledges that the entire message has been heard accurately, then the Receiver can move on to validating.

PART II: **Validating**

EXERCISE

Learning to Validate

Time: 30 minutes

OBJECTIVES

- Create safety in your relationship.

- Develop clear communication and deeper emotional connection.

- Understand and validate your partner's point of view, *whether you agree with it or not.*

Validating is the process of indicating to another person that what he or she says is making sense. You are setting aside your own frame of reference and appreciating the logic, the reality, and the worth of another within his or her frame of reference. Your words send the message to your partner that his or her way of looking at things is valid.

To validate your partner's experience *does not* mean that you necessarily agree with your partner, or that his or her thoughts and feelings reflect your own. It means that you surrender your place at the center of and source of "truth" and allow space for your partner's interpretation of reality. When you mirror and validate your partner, you are setting up the conditions that allow him or her to meet basic needs for self-expression. As a result, the trust and closeness between you will grow.

STEP 1.

The Receiver validates the Sender's message by beginning with one of the following sentence stems: "You make sense, because . . ." or "It makes sense to me, given that you . . ." or "I can see what you are saying . . ."

EXAMPLE:

Using the example of Bill and Barbara above, Bill might validate what Barbara has just told him by saying, "I can see what you are saying. It's so beautiful out. It makes sense that you would want to do some gardening." This response indicates that Bill understands the logic of what Barbara is saying. It acknowledges Barbara's "truth."

This example is so neutral that there isn't much that Bill and Barbara can take issue with. Most of the time, though, dialogue is used to talk about issues that are more emotional or full of conflict. The challenge for the Receiver is to remember that it doesn't matter whether he or she agrees with the Sender or not. What matters is that the Receiver acknowledges the logic or "truth" of the Sender's experience. The message *has to be* that the Sender is not illogical or crazy. Therefore, it is useful to use the phrase "makes sense" to indicate when you are validating.

STEP 2.

The Receiver should check to see if the Sender feels validated by asking, "Do you feel that I have validated you?" If so, then the Receiver moves on to empathy, the final step.

PART III: Empathizing

EXERCISE

Learning to Show Empathy

Time: 30 minutes

OBJECTIVES

- Create safety in your relationship.

- Develop clear communication and deeper emotional connection.

- Express empathy for your partner's feelings.

Empathizing is the process of recognizing the feelings of another person while he or she is expressing a point of view or telling a story. There are two levels of empathy. On the first level, we reflect on and imagine the feelings another person is expressing. On the second and deeper level, we experience emotionally—actually feeling—what he or she is experiencing.

Such empathic experiences are healing and transforming in and of themselves, *independent of what is being communicated*. During these moments, both participants transcend their separateness and experience a genuine meeting of minds and hearts. When you engage in dialogue with your partner, you understand your partner, and at least for a moment, you see the world through his or her eyes.

STEP 1.

Empathy can be expressed with the following sentence stem: "I can imagine that you might be feeling . . ." If the Sender's report is about the past, the Receiver can say: "I can imagine that you might have felt . . ." These sentence stems can be used if the Sender has not openly expressed feelings. If the Sender has expressed feelings, then the Receiver can say: "I can see that you are feeling . . ." Feelings are best stated using one word, such as angry, sad, upset, happy, and so on. If you use more than one word, such as "you feel you don't want to go to work," you are probably expressing a thought.

EXAMPLE:

Although Jack does not want his wife Emily to stop being a stay-at-home mom and return to work, he demonstrates that he is sensitive to how she is experiencing full-time parenting. He says, "I can see how trapped you are feeling at home these days. You must be missing the camaraderie and challenge of working."

STEP 2.

Since one never knows for sure what another person is feeling, it is important to check for accuracy by saying, "Is that what you are feeling?" or, "Did I get your feeling right?" If the Receiver did not imagine the right feeling or misperceived the expressed feeling, then the Sender should say what he or she *is* feeling. Also, if the Sender shares other feelings that were not picked up by the Receiver, the Receiver should mirror those feelings and ask, "Is there more about those feelings?"

> *EXAMPLE:*
>
> *Jack, from the previous example, wants to check to see whether his perceptions of Emily's feelings are on target or not. He says, "I want to be sure that I am understanding you correctly. Am I right that you wish you were back in your old office with your friends?" After Emily responds to his question, he gives her the chance to elaborate, by saying, "Is there more you want to tell me about this?"*

PART IV: **Taking Turns**

<u>EXERCISE</u>

Trading Places

Time: 60–90 minutes

OBJECTIVES

- Create safety in your relationship.

- Develop clear communication and deeper emotional connection.

- Practice and reinforce your skills by working from different perspectives.

STEP 1.

When the Receiver has mirrored, validated, and empathized, the partners exchange roles. The Receiver indicates he or she has something to communicate by saying, "I would like to respond now." Then the Receiver becomes the Sender, and the Sender becomes the Receiver. The Sender (former Receiver) may respond to the message he or she heard, or may express feelings or thoughts about something entirely different. The same three processes of mirroring, validating, and empathizing are repeated until the Sender is satisfied he or she has been heard and understood.

STEP 2.

When it's your turn to listen, give your partner your full attention. Mirror what your partner is saying until you get it. Then validate her or his point of view and communicate empathy. You may ask clarifying questions, but do not try to analyze your partner, make interpretations, or express frustrations or criticisms. As you listen, try to visualize your partner's issues with giving and receiving.

When it's your turn to speak, you are giving yourself to your partner and helping him or her to become larger by taking in your reality. There is security in knowing that you will have the opportunity to express your thoughts and feelings as many times as it takes for your partner to hear and understand you.

BETWEEN-SESSION ASSIGNMENTS

It takes a long time to learn and be comfortable with the Imago Dialogue. The more you practice, the more natural this form of communication will become. Every time you practice the Imago Dialogue, you have a choice about how to arrange it. You can do all three steps of mirroring, validating, and empathizing in the same practice session, or you can practice mirroring in one session, and validating and empathizing in a separate session.

- After you have completed this session, set a goal of engaging in at least one additional dialogue during this week that is not related to the other exercises in this workbook. Choose a neutral subject for this dialogue. A neutral subject, such as what happened in your day, or what you hope to accomplish during the day, allows you to focus your attention on practicing the *form* of dialogue without being distracted by emotional content.
- You will be using the Imago Dialogue to share what you and your partner are learning from the other sessions in this workbook. Besides focusing on form, your attention will be on the information and the feelings of your partner's reality. Stretch yourself toward being open to your partner's experience without interference from your own ideas and judgments.
- At least once this week, share with your partner what you have added to your Daily Gift Record. See Session 1, page 20 for instructions. In addition, at least once this week, share with your partner what you have written down on your partner's Dream Gift List. See page 22 for instructions.

Learning How You Know

REVIEW IN *RECEIVING LOVE*

> **Introduction,** "Learning to Know More Completely," pages 8–12
>
> **Chapter 8,** "Separate and Connected Knowing," pages 174–177
>
> **Chapter 9,** "Practice Relational Knowing," pages 183–185

TIME FRAME

Part I, approximately 15 minutes

Part II or III, approximately 1 hour

SPECIAL CONSIDERATIONS

This session asks you to think about an aspect of your functioning you may never have considered before. Depending on how comfortable you are with introspection, you may find yourself needing to take more time to answer these questions. The effort will be worth it. Ultimately, the goal of this, and the other sessions in this workbook, is to help you become more whole as a person, with a broader range of options at your command.

WHAT YOU NEED TO KNOW

Most of the time we are concerned about *what* we know. Seldom do we consider *how* we know what we know. This exercise is designed to help you become aware of two ways of knowing, called separate and connected knowing. It will help you discover how you tend to process information.

Separate knowing consists of learning and recalling facts, forming thoughts, and analyzing information. It is "head" work. This is what most people think of when they think about knowing. But connected knowing is an equally valid way of knowing that centers on comprehension through intuition and feelings. Connected knowing is "heart" work.

All of us use both kinds of knowing. We were born with the capacity to do both. However, as a result of our childhood experiences and natural pre-disposition, we come to rely on one kind of knowing at the expense of the other. Either we almost always want to *stick with the facts,* or we almost always want to *feel our way through* situations. We don't develop our innate capacities for both kinds of knowing, and, as a consequence, we don't approach our daily lives with all of our faculties for absorbing and accessing information and experiences.

PART I: Are You a Separate or Connected Knower?

EXERCISE

Are You a Separate or Connected Knower?

Time: 15 minutes

OBJECTIVE

• To learn whether you are primarily a separate or a connected knower.

STEP 1.

To help you better understand the difference between separate and connected knowing, read through the statements below that define each one. Put a check mark beside the statements that describe your way of receiving information. Study each statement carefully and think about how it applies to you. Do you tend to approach new information as a separate knower or a connected knower?

To get a sense of which mode of knowing you primarily rely on, imagine a situation where your partner is telling you why he or she believes in a course of action that runs counter to your expectations. For example, suppose that the two of you had been assuming you would go to your partner's high school reunion, and now your partner doesn't want to go. Or, imagine that the two of you had talked about sending your son to private school, and now your partner is telling you that he or she wants to enroll your son in public school. Or, imagine that you've always gone to your parents' house for Christmas, and now your partner says he or she doesn't want to go this year.

SEPARATE KNOWING

You have an exaggerated reliance on *separate knowing* when you:

_____ 1. Listen to what others are saying with a critical ear.

_____ 2. Examine arguments analytically, looking for flaws in the reasoning, insisting that every point be justified.

_____ 3. Take an adversarial stance toward the ideas of others, even when the ideas seem appealing.

_____ 4. Do not see the other person and what he or she is saying as unique, but see that person as an instance of a category or genre.

—— 5. Do not enter into the experience of the other person and imagine yourself in that person's place.

—— 6. Are most comfortable when the other person is responding to you on the basis of the impersonal, cognitive content of your ideas and not on an emotional basis.

Other clues that you are a *separate knower* exist when other people notice that you:

—— 7. Speak clearly, succinctly, and logically, but with little if any *affect* (visible, nonverbal communication).

—— 8. Are impatient when other people elaborate their points excessively.

—— 9. Do not convey warmth or sympathy.

CONNECTED KNOWING
You have exaggerated reliance on *connected* knowing when you:

—— 1. Listen with an empathic, receptive ear.

—— 2. Do not demand that other people justify what they are saying.

—— 3. Wonder to yourself, when you disagree with what's being said, *What in their experience has led them to that point of view?*

—— 4. Want to understand what is being said instead of testing its validity.

—— 5. Try to embrace new ideas, looking for what makes sense even in positions that seem initially wrongheaded or abhorrent.

—— 6. Are willing to enter into stories beyond the bounds of your own experience and attempt to find meaning in narratives that, at first blush, make little sense.

—— 7. Are not comfortable when people respond to you, not with a sense of shared understanding, but primarily with analyses, solutions, and other impersonal approaches.

Other clues that you are a *connected knower* exist when other people can observe that:

—— 8. You cannot say what you mean succinctly.

—— 9. Your partner and others become impatient with your elaborations.

——10. Your partner and others say that you get overly emotional.

STEP 2.

The statements above are meant to give you a sense of which mode of knowing is the one you operate within most often, and the extent to which you have an exaggerated reliance on one mode over the other.

Count up the number of check marks you have in each category. Their distribution will indicate whether you are primarily a separate or connected knower. If almost all your check marks are under separate knowing, then you are primarily a separate knower. If, on the other hand, they are mostly under connected knowing, then you are primarily a connected knower. If they are about equal in each category, then you have more of a balance between the two and are a *relational* knower, someone who uses both kinds of knowing to learn about your environment.

The Knowing Scale below will help you make your self-assessment less general and more concrete. SK stands for "separate knowing" and CK stands for "connected knowing." Using your responses to the sentences above as a guide, make a judgment about what kind of knowing you use most often. As you consider each of the sentences, if you think you are a separate knower, give yourself a rating of 1–4 on the SK side of the scale. If you think you are a connected knower, give yourself a rating of 1–4 on the CK side of the scale. These numbers represent the degree to which you think you manifest this trait. The number "1" indicates that you think you are strongly one way or the other; the number "4" indicates that you think you are weakly one way or the other. The closer your rating is to the center (number "5"), the closer you are to being a relational knower.

SK	1	2	3	4	5	4	3	2	1	CK

STEP 3.

Ask your partner for an Imago Dialogue to discuss how you would rate each other on the Knowing Scale. Does your partner think of you primarily as a separate knower or a connected knower? How does this assessment differ from your own? If you do not have a partner, you might ask a close friend to rate you and compare your ratings to your friend's.

Bringing separate and connected knowing into balance will deepen your ability to experience life. Your relationships will improve, your choices will be better informed, and your functioning will be enhanced. When you can move easily from separate to connected knowing as the situation demands, you are engaging in what we call "relational knowing." Relational knowing depends on the integration of both ways of knowing as they combine in a way that serves you best.

The exercises that follow will help separate knowers develop their connected knowing skills and connected knowers develop their separate knowing skills. After you have determined which kind of knowing is dominant for you, select the growth process that will help you expand your skills. The goal is to become comfortable using a full range of faculties for assimilating new information and deepening your understanding of situations and relationships. If you are a separate knower, go to "Part II: Growth Process for Separate Knowers," immediately following. If you are a connected knower, go to "Part III: Growth Process for Connected Knowers," page 44.

PART II: Growth Process for Separate Knowers

EXERCISE

Develop Your Connected Knowing Skills

Time: 1 hour

OBJECTIVES

- To become a relational knower.

- To keep your separate knowing skill, but at the same time increase your connected knowing skill.

- To become more familiar and intimate with your inner world of feelings, images, intuitions, and hunches.

- To develop your ability to speak your feelings and be an empathic listener for others.

STEP 1.

Practice becoming silent inside. Listen to your breath as you breathe in and out in a normal rhythm. Let yourself become aware of any muscle tightness you might be holding on to in your neck, your shoulders, your arms, your hands, your chest, your belly, your legs, or your feet. With your next breath out, let the muscle tightness leave your body. Next, become aware of whatever thoughts, feelings, or visual images you may be experiencing. Let them go as you breathe out. You are clear and clean inside, empty of whatever fears, judgments, and worries you usually carry with you. You are open to receiving whatever your partner wants to offer you.

STEP 2.

Practice becoming present to others. Invite your partner to share something with you, either informally or using the Imago Dialogue process you learned in Session 2. To deepen your resonance with your partner's experience, place your hand over your partner's heart and experience his or her body sensations. Release any thoughts, analyses, suggestions, solutions, and judgments, and allow your partner to be who he or she is. Become curious about your partner's feelings, and make space in your consciousness for his or her reality. Imagine that your partner's experience is happening to you. Allow yourself to respond with empathy.

STEP 3.

Practice being present to your emotional self. Find a quiet place where you will not be disturbed, and sit quietly. Allow yourself to become aware of your feelings, intuitions, hunches, body sensations, and any visual images that may arise. You want to welcome these aspects of yourself into your awareness. You want to *be* with them without censor. Whenever your focus is interrupted by thoughts, analyses, suggestions, solutions, or judgments, notice that you are having them, and then let them go. Gently return to experiencing your inner world.

STEP 4.

Practice translating actions into words and feelings. The next time you become aware of wanting to take a particular action, such as getting up from your chair, taking a drink, eating, or going to find your partner, let yourself pause first. Rather than simply acting, notice what you are feeling and thinking in connection with your proposed action. Put your feelings and thoughts into words to yourself. Tell yourself what you want to do, why you want to do it, how you feel at this moment, and then decide whether you want to proceed with the action or not.

STEP 5.

Practice processing your emotions. Ask your partner for an Imago Dialogue. Tell your partner that you simply want to practice putting your feelings into words. Then, for 15 minutes, tell your partner how you felt when a particular event happened in the past, or how you are feeling now as you are talking. Go as deeply into these feelings as you can, suspending any thoughts, analyses, or judgments that you might have. Ask your partner to mirror your feelings until the mirror accurately reflects what you've said.

Here are some sentence stems that can help you talk about your feelings:

- When we got up this morning, I felt . . .
- By the end of the day, I was feeling . . .
- When I think back over the last week, I realize I felt most (happy, sad, angry, worried) on this occasion . . .
- The thing I'm most looking forward to is this . . . , because it makes me feel this . . . when I think about it.
- The last time we (went out alone together, saw your family, went to church, went shopping together, watched TV together, had dinner at home together, slept in, talked about the family budget), I felt this . . .

Another way to practice expressing your feelings is by positive flooding. (See Session 5 for more information.) You can flood your partner or a friend with all the positive feelings you have about them and your relationship with them. When you are finished, ask your partner or friend to mirror your feelings.

STEP 6.

Practice experiencing the energy of your heart. Find a quiet place where you know you won't be disturbed. Shut your eyes and focus on your breathing—in and out, in and out. Listen to the sound your breath makes, feel your body fill with air, and then feel your body contract. Now, let yourself imagine that your brain is so powerful that it creates an energy field that radiates out into your environment. You can imagine your brain power as light that spreads clarity and wisdom into the darkness. You know you can rely on your intelligence to help you understand your experience. You know you can take problems apart by analyzing them and putting them back together in a logical way.

Now, shift your focus to your heart. Can you isolate what your heart, as a special organ in your body, feels like at this moment? Imagine that the warmth and empathy from your heart radiate energy outward into your environment. Your compassion and understanding are so powerful that they touch the lives of everyone around you. You know that you can rely on your feelings to help you understand your experience. You know that you have the ability to put yourself into the shoes of others to see what they're seeing, feel what they're feeling—and that this ability will help you solve problems and overcome obstacles.

Let yourself stay in this state of heart energy for as long as you can. And then again become aware of your breathing in and out. Slowly open your eyes and smile at how satisfying it was to experience the power you have to be comfortable with your feelings and your compassion.

PART III: Growth Process for Connected Knowers

<u>**EXERCISE**</u>

Develop Your Separate Knowing Skills

Time: 1 hour

OBJECTIVES

- To become a relational knower.

- To keep your connected knowing skill, but at the same time increase your separate knowing skill.

- To become more familiar with your thoughts, analytic skills, logical-sequential thinking, and ability to solve problems.

- To develop your ability to think clearly, speak succinctly, and enjoy the external world.

STEP 1.

Practice becoming silent inside. Listen to your breath as you breathe in and out in a normal rhythm. Let yourself become aware of any muscle tightness you might be holding on to in your neck, your shoulders, your arms, your hands, your chest, your belly, your legs, or your feet. With your next breath out, let the muscle tightness leave your body. Next, become aware of whatever thoughts, feelings, or visual images you may be experiencing. Let them go as you breathe out. You are clear and clean inside, empty of whatever fears, judgments, and worries you usually carry with you. You are open to receiving whatever your partner wants to offer you.

STEP 2.

Practice keeping your partner's feelings separate from your own. Invite your partner to share something with you, either informally or using the Imago Dialogue process you learned in Session 2. To deepen your resonance with your partner's experience, place your hand over your partner's heart and experience his or her body sensations. Release any thoughts, analyses, suggestions, solutions, and judgments, and allow your partner to be who he or she is. Become curious about your partner's feelings, and make space in your consciousness for his or her reality. Let yourself become aware that your partner's feelings belong to your partner, whether they are the same as yours or not. Stay aware of your partner's separateness at the same time that you register his or her feelings.

STEP 3.

Practice being present to your rational self. Find a quiet place where you will not be disturbed, and sit quietly. Allow yourself to become aware of your thoughts. When a thought does arise, allow yourself to pick up the thread and follow it until it crystallizes into words. Encourage yourself to construct a logical argument, look for facts that can support your point of view, and emphasize rational step-by-step progression through your analysis. Hold your thought or your argument in your mind for a few moments. If a feeling or intuition arises, notice it, but gently go back to using your reasoning faculties.

STEP 4.

Practice finding the thoughts behind your feelings. Allow yourself to surface a feeling about something important to you. Then consciously form one clear, succinct thought on this subject. Become aware of the places your thought becomes diffuse or fuzzy. Challenge yourself to become focused on that part of your thought. Imagine that you are required to present your line of thinking in a logical way to another person. How would you state your argument? When feelings, images, intuitions, and hunches intrude, let them go, and return your attention to your rational thinking process.

STEP 5.

Practice translating feelings into words and actions. Become aware of the next time you have a strong feeling about your partner or one of your partner's behaviors. Rather than staying in your feelings, initiate a dialogue with your partner. Ask him or her to listen to you as you explain logically and succinctly how you feel. Ask your partner to mirror what you have said. How well your partner mirrors not only says something about his or her capacity to listen accurately, it also gives you information about how clearly you can convey your message.

Continue this practice in clear thinking by asking your partner for the behavior change you desire. Be specific about what you want by making the behavior measurable and time-limited. Notice how it feels to put your feelings into words clearly enough to be fully understood.

Here are some statements to help you talk about your thoughts:

- I had some strong feelings when you said *this* to me, and now I'd like to analyze what lies behind my feelings.
- I realize that I have been unhappy with the way we are approaching *this* issue. I would like to suggest that we do things differently. What would you think if I did this (new behavior) instead? If you think that's a good idea, then I would like to ask for your help. How would you feel about doing this (new behavior) along with me? Let's set a trial time of one month for our new behaviors. We can then have a dialogue to analyze how they are working or not working.

- Instead of just ranting about this, I've decided to break the problem down into parts. I'm going to look for something concrete I can do to address one of these smaller parts.
- I want to tell you why I feel so (happy, sad, angry, worried). I can trace my feelings back to earlier experiences and see the bridge between what happened in the past and why I have these feelings now.

STEP 6.

Practice containing your emotions. Find a quiet place, and let yourself experience your feelings around a problem, imagining energy circling your heart. Then imagine that energy shifting to your mind, circling it with a warm glow, and radiating out toward the problem you would like to solve. Use the energy that your mind is generating to construct a plan for addressing the problem. Envision yourself carrying out the plan. Then, ask yourself how it feels to approach the problem with a doable, self-generated, concrete plan for addressing it.

STEP 7.

Practice experiencing the energy of your mind. Find a quiet place where you know you won't be disturbed. Shut your eyes and focus on your breathing—in and out, in and out. Listen to the sound your breath makes, feel your body fill with air, and then feel your body contract. Now, let yourself imagine that the emotional power generated from your heart is so strong that it creates an energy field radiating out into your environment. You can imagine that this ability to know through your feelings and intuition is a light that spreads clarity and wisdom into the darkness. You know you can rely on your emotional intelligence to help you understand your experience. You know you can solve problems by feeling your way through them, understanding what it means to see the world in a different way, and relying on your gut feelings as a guide to the best solution.

Now, shift your focus to your mind. Can you isolate what your brain, as a special organ in your body, feels like at this moment? Imagine that your brain is growing in its reasoning and thinking power. You have the ability to sort out confusing situations and learn the facts in challenging situations. Your intelligence and capacity to get to the bottom of things is so powerful that they touch the lives of everyone around you. You know that you can rely on your mind to help you understand your experience. You know that you have the ability to think logically and rationally in every situation—and that this ability will help you solve problems and overcome obstacles.

Let yourself stay in this state of mind energy for as long as you can. And then again become aware of your breathing in and out. Slowly open your eyes and smile at how satisfying it was to experience the power you have to be comfortable with your ability to think and reason.

Just being aware that there are different ways to know about relationships and the other realities in your life will help you become intentional about using both separate and connected knowing. Remember that the more balanced your ways of knowing are, the more of yourself you are able to bring to your relationships, and the fuller, happier, and more conscious your connections with others will be. It is challenging to know another person. To do so in a real way, you have to use both separate and connected knowing skills.

BETWEEN-SESSION ASSIGNMENTS

Just learning about separate and connected knowing is useful for understanding which of your natural capacities you are not developing. But to make changes toward the balance you are striving for, you have to catch yourself in the act of relying on one mode of knowing and neglecting the other.

- At least once each week, let your partner know that you noticed yourself using either separate or connected knowing to the exclusion of the other. Then, ask your partner to listen while you discuss the same event, idea, feelings, or problem from the other mode of knowing.
- Continue to make entries in your Gift Diary notebook as discussed in Session 1, pages 16–19. Taking a few minutes every day to note the many gifts you receive in your life will help you live in an atmosphere of abundance. In addition, engage your partner in at least one Imago Dialogue this week. You are still learning this important skill and practice is essential. Be alert for a topic that has medium-level emotional content, something you care about, but not something that is so emotional your heart races and your blood pressure rises when you think of it. You will probably want to refresh yourself about the specific steps involved in Imago Dialogue in Session 2 (see pages 26–32).

Practice Receiving and Giving

REVIEW IN *RECEIVING LOVE*

Chapter 1, "Yes . . . But," pages 28–30

Chapter 2, "An Expanded Idea of Relationship," pages 32–37

Chapter 5, "The Partner Who Can't Receive," pages 119–122, "The Partner Who Is Trying to Give," pages 122–123, "Giving and Receiving Are Part of the Same System," pages 123–126

Chapter 7, "Learning to Receive," pages 144–160

TIME FRAME

Between 1 hour and 1 hour and 30 minutes

SPECIAL CONSIDERATIONS

This session begins by helping you expand your capacity to recognize the basic gifts of life we have all been given, and then it builds upon the skills you are gaining in Imago Dialogue by asking you to share your experiences of structured giving and receiving with your partner. You will need relaxed, unhurried time to take in the sensations that are highlighted in each exercise, and then to share them when asked to.

PART I: Receiving Sensory Impressions

WHAT YOU NEED TO KNOW

The following tasks are designed to assist you in developing your capacity to receive. Receiving is a prerequisite to giving. Learning to receive enlarges the self and empowers others.

There is a correlation between self-rejection and the inability to receive love. Our unconscious cannot accept avowals of love for parts of us we hate or don't know we have, even when those parts reflect positive traits. In order for us to receive the love of others, we have to work through our self-rejection in concert with a marriage partner or another intimate partner committed to consciousness. In a relationship of this kind, we can learn to love in another person what we have rejected in ourselves.

When a parent rejects or tries to stifle a natural impulse or a natural function in a child, we can see the birth of self-rejection. The child will do anything he can to protect himself from parental rejection. He will even hate the parts of himself that imperil his parents' love and cause them to reject him. To the child, rejection equals abandonment, and abandonment equals death. He must do what he can to survive.

It is useful to describe this as a sequence: The child manifests some perfectly natural impulse through actions, the parent reacts with disapproval, the child registers the impulse as bad and dangerous, and he hates himself for having it. He unconsciously shuts down that rejected part of himself and loses contact with it.

As adults, we bring this self-rejection we learned in childhood into our intimate relationships. As a result, we tend to become self-absorbed and shut down our five senses. We do not take in sensations from our physical environment. Although we are all dependent upon this environment, self-preoccupation does not allow us to experience the gift of sensation nor experience the awareness of our dependency.

EXERCISE

Learning to Appreciate Your Senses

Time: 15–30 minutes

OBJECTIVES

- To recapture what you have lost from your five senses.

- To experience the world around you more fully.

If it is difficult, in general, for you to receive love, it can be helpful to practice receiving something that is simple and concrete. That's why this exercise focuses on taking in the sensory experiences that are available to all of us every day. Experiencing and accepting what you can smell, see, touch, hear, and taste will help you learn how to accept the more complex ways your partner gives to you.

To reactivate your sensory organs, you need to practice paying attention to the stimuli that come in from your environment. The following exercise will help you recognize and appreciate the scents, sights, textures, sounds, and tastes that are always around you, waiting for you to let them in.

The best way to do this exercise is to go outside with your partner and walk around. When you are outside:

1. Just breathe. Be aware only of the air coming in and out through your nostrils. Take a deep breath in and let the air out. Receive the air. Say to yourself, "I am breathing in the air. It's just there and it's there for me."

   After a few moments of being aware of breathing in the air, engage your partner in a brief exercise of communicating and listening. Although this is based on Imago Dialogue and is definitely in the spirit of Imago Dialogue, the two of you will focus on sending and receiving communication, without explicitly mirroring, validating, and empathizing.

   Invite your partner to be the Sender and to tell you how it was for him or her to breathe and be aware of breathing. As your partner sends you this message, breathe in the words in the same way you breathed in the air. Let your partner's words and emotions come in and become part of you. Then offer to be the Sender and give your partner the chance to be the Receiver in the same spirit of total acceptance.

2. Now, as you continue breathing, let yourself notice how the air smells. Close your eyes and see if you can identify the aromas in the air. Turn slowly around and try to distinguish differences in what you can smell. Is there a prevailing aroma? If so, is it pleasant or unpleasant? Does it call to mind other experiences?

   In the spirit of dialogue, invite your partner to be the Sender and to tell you how it was for him or her to become aware of the way the air smells. As your partner sends you this message, take in the words in the same way you welcomed in the sensation of smell.

3. Next, allow yourself to look around and really see what is in front of you. See as specifically and as completely as you can. What are the details of the grass? What are the lines and color variations that make up the crack in the sidewalk? Be aware of the images coming in through your eyes. Let them in. Let yourself see the colors of the trees, grass, and flowers; the movement of the birds; and the clouds floating in the sky. Look at your partner. Take in your partner's appearance, the color of his or her eyes, her or his height, and size.

   In the spirit of dialogue, invite your partner to be the Sender and to tell you how it was for him or her to see and be aware of seeing. As your partner sends you this message, take in the words in the same way you welcomed in the visual images in your environment. Let your partner's words and emotions become part of you. Then offer to be the Sender and give your partner the chance to be the Receiver in the same spirit of total acceptance.

4. Allow yourself to become sensitive to touching various objects around you. Reach out and touch a tree, a blade of grass, a rock, or your partner's skin. Experience the sensations on your fingertips. Let these sensations in. Let yourself register the texture, the temperature, and the hardness or softness of what you are feeling.

   In the spirit of dialogue, invite your partner to be the Sender and to tell you how it was for him or her to touch and become aware of the physical sensations of touching various objects. As your partner sends you this message, take in the words in the same way you welcomed in the sensation of touch. Let your partner's words and emotions become part of you. Then offer to be the Sender and give your partner the chance to be the Receiver in the same spirit of total acceptance.

5. Allow yourself to attune your ears to the sounds around you. Listen attentively to whatever sounds are in your environment. Perhaps a breeze is blowing, or there is traffic noise, or there are birds calling in the trees, or people are talking. Can you hear your partner? Can you hear yourself breathing?

   In the spirit of dialogue, invite your partner to be the Sender and to tell you how it was for him or her to listen and be aware of hearing. As your partner sends you this message, take in the words in the same way you welcomed in the sounds in your environment. Let your partner's words and emotions become part of you. Then offer to be the Sender and give your partner the chance to be the Receiver in the same spirit of total acceptance.

6. Allow yourself the sensation of tasting. Focus only on the sensations on your tongue. Experience where the taste sensations go in your body. Taste a piece of fruit or a piece of candy, taste your own skin, or kiss your partner, and taste his or her lips with your tongue. Let yourself taste all of the flavors—sweet, salty, bitter, and sour.

   In the spirit of dialogue, invite your partner to be the Sender and to tell you how it was for him or her to taste and be aware of tasting. As your partner sends you this message, take in the words in the same way you welcomed in the sensations of taste. Let your partner's words and emotions become part of you. Then offer to be the Sender and give your partner the chance to be the Receiver in the same spirit of total acceptance.

7. Now take the experience one step further. Say aloud: "I appreciate the scents around me, the images given to my eyes, the sensations of touch, the sounds, and the tastes I've just experienced." Think of everything in your environment, including your partner, as a gift, and experience the joy of receiving.

PART II: Receiving Your Partner's Reality

WHAT YOU NEED TO KNOW

The goal of Imago Relationship Therapy is to help people break free from their preset ideas and unconscious reactions by becoming more aware of what they actually think and do. Equally important is being able to assess the *meaning* of what they or their partners are doing. Being conscious means being able to ask and answer questions, such as: "Why do I (or you) do that?" "What is it that I am (or you are) trying to accomplish?" "Is there a better way to get this job done?" Or, to put it in the purest form: "What is true?" When you can begin to answer these questions, you can break the grip that habit and conditioning have had on your life. You will be free to consider a range of personal options, including the option of continuing to do what you're doing *or* to modify, eliminate, or replace your old behavior with something more effective.

There are essentially two tasks involved in becoming more conscious: (1) getting more information about your own and your partner's formative histories, childhood wounds, motivations, dreams, and needs, and (2) learning how to interpret what is happening in your relationship in a systematic and meaningful way. The first task is accomplished partly by becoming an opportunist and looking for openings to ask about your partner's life, and then listening to the answers. In addition, completing the sessions in this workbook, and in the *Getting the Love You Want Workbook: The New Couples' Study Guide* will help you become adept at seeing below the surface to the major currents that have shaped you and your partner as individuals. You can accomplish the second task by assessing the significance of what is happening in your relationship, and by becoming a better observer of your own life. Imago Relationship Therapy concepts can help you clarify what you're seeing.

The task of becoming conscious can be accomplished successfully by anyone who wants to undertake the effort. You can choose to interact with your partner mindfully and with self-control. You can achieve a more profound understanding of the processes at work in your relationship. Every relationship pattern takes two people to shape it, but one person alone *can* stimulate growth in a new direction.

EXERCISE

Learning to Appreciate Your Partner

Time: 15–30 minutes

OBJECTIVES

- To see the world through another's eyes.

- To experience the reality of your partner rather than your preconceived idea of him or her.

The last exercise gave you practice in acknowledging and taking in sensations and experiences that were in your physical environment and outside yourself. That exercise was preparation for learning how to understand and absorb the thoughts, feelings, and points of view of another human being, which is much more challenging and complex than learning to taste a peach or see a blade of grass.

In this exercise, you will have the opportunity to be more closely in touch with who your partner really is. What follows are suggestions for an Imago Dialogue that move from sharing about a neutral subject (the exercise you both participated in above) to sharing about a subject that holds more emotion, and more potential for conflict or hurt feelings. Complete this exercise in the same spirit of curiosity and acceptance as you did the last one.

STEP 1.

Find a place where you and your partner can have an uninterrupted dialogue. Invite your partner to be the Sender and to talk about his or her experience of letting in the sensory sensations during the previous exercise. As the Receiver, listen carefully, focusing on your partner's words, tone of voice, and emotions. Let the words and the nonverbal information your partner is sending into your awareness. Allow yourself to experience your partner's inner world. When your own thoughts and feelings come to consciousness, acknowledge them, and then let them go. Let yourself be silent inside, except for what your partner is filling you with.

When your partner has finished sending his or her message, mirror, validate, and empathize using the structure of Imago Dialogue described in Session 2.

STEP 2.

Now change places so that you are the Sender and your partner is the Receiver. Tell your partner what it was like for you to let in the sensory experiences you had during the first exercise. Ask your partner to listen to you with the same complete attention that you listened with.

When you have finished, your partner can mirror, validate, and empathize with what you have just said.

STEP 3.

Now, to deepen your capacity to take in your partner's reality, ask your partner to become the Sender again. This time, invite your partner to tell you about something that is uncomfortable to him or her in your relationship. Because this message may be more difficult to hear than others we have practiced, you may have to remind yourself to stay focused on receiving. Learning how to receive "complaints" is an important step in improving your communication. Your goal is to take in what your partner is saying, regardless of how you feel about it. A person who feels heard will be less angry and frustrated than one who doesn't. Besides, when you do a good job of hearing uncomfortable messages from your partner, you can expect your partner will do the same for you.

Remember that the Sender uses "I" messages when sending a message. As the Receiver, you will want to empty yourself of your own thoughts and feelings and focus on taking in your partner's words and body language, just as you did when the message was more neutral. Let your partner's reality be all that is in your mind. Listen until you are silent inside, and are aware only of your partner's experience.

When your partner has said all he or she wishes to say, mirror, validate, and empathize with what your partner has told you. When your partner is satisfied that you have heard and understood, say to him or her, "I appreciate your sharing your reality with me."

STEP 4.

Switch roles. You are now the Sender and your partner is now the Receiver. Tell your partner about something that makes you uncomfortable about your relationship. Your partner will then mirror, validate, and empathize with you until you are satisfied that you have been heard and understood.

When you have said all you wish to say and you are satisfied that your partner has received your message, then your partner can say to you, "I appreciate your sharing your reality with me."

PART III: Receiving a Gift and Giving a Gift

WHAT YOU NEED TO KNOW

As long as there is self-rejection, we cannot love ourselves, nor can we accept love from others. The path to self-love is to stretch beyond our usual comfort levels to love in our partner what we reject in ourselves. But how can we do this? First, by seeing that the part of our partner that we dislike is really a projection of a part of ourselves that we dislike. Second, by seeing that this trait or behavior helps our partner survive, just as it has helped us survive. We have to see and understand that the "negative" trait serves a positive function. Third, we must then accept that the trait is functional in our partner, and we must come to value it for the purpose it serves. When we understand, accept, and eventually love it in our partner, we come to understand, accept, and love it in ourselves. This is the path of self-acceptance and self-love: *What I do for my partner is done also for me.*

When you are freely able to accept a gift from your partner, you are demonstrating that you acknowledge and appreciate the part of you that is being gifted. Conversely, if you are not able to accept a gift, then you are demonstrating that there is part of you that you still disown or deny. Stretching toward the gift, even when you are initially uncomfortable, allows you to reach toward the part of you that has been denied or disowned, and pull it toward you.

On the other side, it can also be hard to fulfill a request your partner has made. If our partner is asking for something that embodies a quality we don't acknowledge in ourselves, then it can be hard to give it to our partner, because (as we've said) what we give to our partner we are also giving to ourselves. How can we give ourselves something that represents a quality we have denied or disowned? An example is the difficulty Janice had giving her husband the riding mower he had asked for. She insisted that they had always mowed the grass with a push mower and she didn't see any reason to change it. It wasn't the money that stopped Janice. She simply couldn't acknowledge that she and her husband were getting older, and that he needed help to keep up their large property. A series of realizations brought Janice to accept that they were aging, and that the riding mower was merely a convenience, and not a threat to their character or their way of life.

One of the advantages to being in a committed relationship is the freedom and safety it can offer. You and your partner are free to recognize and appreciate your true selves. Being able to give and receive openly teaches partners how to become more whole, and it is a sign that they are *becoming* more whole. Until you have a chance to practice being open to receiving and giving in a safe environment, your goal to become more open to receiving and giving is merely a goal.

The parts of the brain involved in cognitive processing and the parts involved in registering emotion must develop patterns of interaction before an abstract goal can become part of your daily living. When you discover by practicing your receiving and giving skills that your partner is less defensive and starts receiving from and giving to *you,* your good idea is suddenly transformed into something you "know" from the inside out. If you do it often enough, your belief that receiving and giving is a good idea will be integrated into your behavior, and the grip of self-rejection will loosen, while your self-acceptance and self-love strengthen.

EXERCISE

Practice Asking for and Receiving a Gift, *and* Giving a Gift

Time: 15–30 minutes

OBJECTIVES

- To begin the reshaping of your thought processes toward the habit of receiving graciously.

- To understand how the ideas of receiving and giving interact with each other.

Step 1 of this exercise will help you be more comfortable asking your partner for what you want and receiving what you want. It can be done with two possible goals in mind. One possibility is that you are asking for something with the expectation that your partner will be able to give it to you. In this case, you are requesting something that is realistic in this moment, and you are expecting that your partner will stretch to meet your request. The second possibility is that you are doing this exercise for the purpose of practicing your ability to ask, rather than with the expectation that your partner will give you what you ask for. Be clear with your partner about which purpose you are trying to accomplish.

STEP 1.

- Find a time and place when you and your partner can have an uninterrupted dialogue. Tell your partner that you want to make a request, and that your purpose is either (1) to practice asking with the positive expectation that your request will be met, or (2) to practice asking with no particular expectation that your request will be met.

    Ask your partner to give you something you've never before asked for. Take your time and think about a deep desire, the fulfillment of a fantasy, or an unfulfilled yearning. It could be a certain kind of kiss, a massage, a physical item, certain words, or an experience—anything you want that you have never asked for. Be aware of any thoughts, feelings, and physical sensations as you ask, but let them go. Focus only on your asking.

- If your partner is not able to give you what you've asked for, he or she can say, "I'm so glad you can ask for what you want. When you ask, it gives me a chance to expand into a larger person. Although I'm not able to fulfill your request at this moment, I will do what I can to grow toward fulfilling your request."

- If your partner *is* able to give you what you've asked for, open yourself to what is being offered. Let any uncomfortable thoughts, feelings, or physical sensations go. Experience yourself receiving. Say to your partner, "I accept this gift. I appreciate what you have given me. It helps me expand in to a larger person."

STEP 2.

Now it is your turn to be the giver and your partner's turn to be the receiver. Follow the same process as in Step 1, but with your roles reversed. Remember that giving stretches you in to new parts of yourself. Focus on opening yourself to your partner's experience of asking and on your experience of stretching toward giving to your partner.

BETWEEN-SESSION ASSIGNMENTS

Every session in this workbook is designed to help you and your partner accept more fully each other's reality. This is central to learning how to receive love.

- Every time you engage in Imago Dialogue this week (excluding those dialogues that are assigned in this workbook), practice the process of accepting your partner's reality as outlined in Part II.
- In addition, at least once each week, practice the exercise "Practice Asking for and Receiving a Gift, *and* Giving a Gift" with your partner.
- Previous Sessions:
    1. Continue making entries in your Daily Gift Record and your Dream Gift List from Session 1, pages 20–23.
    2. Also, observe your tendencies to overemphasize either separate or connected knowing. When you catch yourself doing it, pause for a moment and continue discussing the same event, idea, feeling, or problem from the other mode of knowing. Session 3, which begins on page 35, presents a detailed discussion of separate and connected knowing.

Positive Flooding

REVIEW IN *RECEIVING LOVE*

Chapter 4, "Splitting," pages 74–82

Chapter 6, "Reparative Relationships," pages 136–139

Chapter 7, "The Mirror of the Other," pages 145–147

TIME FRAME

Approximately 30 minutes

SPECIAL CONSIDERATIONS

This session encourages you to let go and express your emotional side. It is an effective way to disrupt habitually negative patterns of interaction with an attention-getting display of positive feeling. If Positive Flooding feels uncomfortable at first, know that the more you do it, the easier and more effective it is in shifting your relationship onto a more positive footing.

WHAT YOU NEED TO KNOW

Simple moments of enjoyment can transform a troubled relationship. Here is a positive exercise partners can do to increase goodwill between them.

We call this the Positive Flooding exercise. The first time you do it, if you are on the receiving end, you may feel suspicious or uncomfortable. It takes time to get used to being appreciated, especially if verbal appreciation hasn't been part of your relationship up to this point. After a few experiences with the exercise, though, you will start internalizing all the wonderful things you are hearing about yourself from your partner. This exercise will give you good practice at giving and receiving, provide a chance to have some fun together, and increase your self-esteem.

Be sure that the receiving partner feels loved and honored. Then, no matter how silly the Sender is being, the underlying feelings of praise and love will come through, accompanied with smiles and laughter. Do not tease or make fun of the Receiver; he or she needs to be able to accept what is offered without complications. Also, it's a good idea for partners to take turns being the Sender and the Receiver. In this way a boomerang effect is created that always brings love back to the one who is giving it out. These moments are powerful. They remind us why we are in a relationship—to give and receive love.

We recommend doing this exercise formally at least once a week. When you are positive flooding, include the traits you value in each other, *and* the traits you both want to have valued. Including the traits you both want to have valued helps each of you to recover lost parts of yourself and to build your relationship's potential for healing. As the exercise becomes more comfortable, you can make informal positive flooding part of your daily interaction, showering each other regularly with words of love and appreciation.

This exercise changes chronic negativity to a pattern of positive appreciation. Each time you engage in this exercise, you are strengthening your ability to give and receive love. Raising your voice while positive flooding increases the emotional intensity with which you express your positive feelings to your partner. Positive words expressed with intense emotions are enough to overcome the defenses your partner may have against receiving love. Over time, verbal appreciation creates safety and joy in your relationship, and every aspect of your lives together improves.

EXERCISE

Learning Positive Flooding

Time: 15 minutes

OBJECTIVES

- To retrain your mind and heart to hear and accept positive things about yourself.

- To have fun together.

STEP 1.

Ask your partner to sit in a chair, and, while walking in a circle around your partner, keep eye contact and say all the positive things you can think of about his or her physical characteristics, character traits, behaviors, talents, abilities, intelligence, creativity, and so forth.

Flood your partner by starting with your voice at its regular volume and then raising it with each one of your positive comments. At the end of the flooding, you should be *shouting* positive global expressions of caring to your partner, such as, "You are the most thoughtful husband in the world!" or, "You are the most wonderful wife in the universe!" Shout these exclamations with a level of intensity equal to your voice level when you are shouting with rage or anger.

STEP 2.

While you are doing this, be aware of reactions on your partner's face and his or her body language.

STEP 3.

Now, ask your partner for an Imago Dialogue about the experience you've both had with this exercise. Ask him or her to talk about how it felt to be positively flooded. Pay particular attention to the words you said that your partner mentally deflected, the words that were let in, and the specific feelings that were elicited in your partner by each comment you made.

STEP 4.

Switch roles. It's now time for your partner to positive flood you.

EXERCISE

Expanding Positive Flooding

Time: 15 minutes

OBJECTIVES

- To recover parts of your lost self.

- To build your relationship's potential for healing.

STEP 1.

In the chart below, write down those aspects of yourself you would like your partner to flood with praise and appreciation. In the Global Affirmations column, include whatever you wished you had heard in your childhood, and whatever you would like to hear from your partner if you had the relationship of your dreams.

Physical Characteristics	Character Traits	Behaviors	Global Affirmations

EXAMPLE:

Danielle filled out her chart this way:

Physical Characteristics	Character Traits	Behaviors	Global Affirmations
I have a beautiful smile.	*I do a good job of loving him.*	*I am a good listener.*	*I am smart.*
I have a strong body.	*He trusts me.*	*I respect his privacy.*	*I am creative.*
He loves my freckles.	*I am competent.*	*I am a good housekeeper.*	*I am a good friend.*

STEP 2.
Ask your partner to repeat the flooding exercise, using the chart you have filled out as a guide.

STEP 3.
Share what it was like for you to experience this positive flooding, based on your own words. Use the Imago Dialogue to structure your discussion of this experience.

STEP 4.
Exchange roles with your partner. Repeat steps 1, 2, and 3, with your partner as the Receiver and you as the Sender. Ask your partner to use the above chart as a guide for writing down how he or she would like to be positively flooded. Flood your partner, using his or her own words, and then ask him or her to share the experience with you, using the Imago Dialogue process.

This simple exercise can provide important clues about where you and your partner have been wounded. If either of you has trouble letting in certain kinds of positive comments, then you know your self-conception has been injured in that place. For example, Susan admitted that it was hard for her to hear that she was a good mother. When she and her husband had an Imago Dialogue about this afterward, she was able to see a connection to a painful incident in her childhood. Susan remembered the guilt she felt when her pet hamster died, partly as a result of carelessness on her part. Although her mother didn't tell her she was going to be a bad mother, Susan definitely took away the feeling that she shouldn't be trusted with other living things to care for.

BETWEEN-SESSION ASSIGNMENTS

- At least once a week, you and your partner should do the Learning Positive Flooding and the Expanding Positive Flooding exercises.
- As you think of them, add to your list of the attributes you would like your partner to acknowledge when he or she does positive flooding for you.
- At least every other time you do this exercise, you and your partner should refer to each other's updated list as a guide for positive flooding.
- Previous Sessions:
  1. From Session 1, continue maintaining the Daily Gift Record and adding to the Dream Gift List, pages 20–23.
  2. From Session 2, observe whether you are still seeing the world predominantly from either separate or connected knowing, and practice discussing thoughts, feelings, or events from the other mode of knowing. Session 2 begins on page 24.
  3. From Session 4, practice the exercise "Practice Asking for and Receiving a Gift, *and* Giving a Gift," page 56.

Your "Receiving Quotient" Assessment

REVIEW IN *RECEIVING LOVE*

    Chapter 1, "The Pattern," pages 27–30

TIME FRAME

30 minutes

SPECIAL CONSIDERATIONS

Session 5 involved letting yourself go and expressing your emotions. This session involves completing a detailed questionnaire. You will have the opportunity to examine your attitudes and behaviors about receiving gifts in a way that you haven't done before. Take your time, and answer as honestly as you can.

WHAT YOU NEED TO KNOW

This session will help you assess how receptive you are to the different kinds of gifts people commonly offer to you, themselves, and others. It will help you pinpoint whether certain kinds of gifts are more difficult for you to receive and/or witness. Sharing your answers with your partner will increase the understanding and empathy you have for each other.

EXERCISE

Examining your Receptivity

Time: 30 minutes

OBJECTIVES

- To begin improving your ability to receive gifts, praise, and love.

- To begin improving your ability to witness others receiving gifts, praise, and love.

STEP 1.

Below are 50 questions designed to help you discover what we are calling your "receiving quotient." Answer how often you do what is stated by marking each item with S for "sometimes," O for "often," or N for "never" or "rarely." The number of Ns will measure your "positive receiving quotient." The number of Ss and Os will measure your "negative receiving quotient."

Take your time thinking about each question. Use your capacities for separate and connected knowing as you respond. Evaluate each statement from a factual perspective, *and* consider each one from a more intuitive, emotional perspective. To get a complete and honest picture of how well you are able to receive and witness receiving, you must call upon your ability to assess yourself from both perspectives.

1._____Do you feel uncomfortable when someone brags about you?

2._____Do you feel critical when someone brags about himself or herself?

3._____Do you feel negative toward someone else who is bragged about by another person?

4._____Do you feel critical when someone lets himself be bragged about?

5._____Do you ever get a gift and feel obligated?

6._____Do you ever get gifts and forget you got them?

7._____Do you ever devalue the gifts others give you?

8._____Do you ever refuse to take gifts?

9._____Do you ever deflect compliments when you get them?

10._____Do you ever ask for something, get it, and find something wrong with it?

11._____Do you ever find yourself mainly remembering only the "bad times"?

12._____Do you ever ask for something, get it, and then forget that you asked for it?

13._____Do you ever ask for something, get it, and then forget that you got it?

14._____Do you ask for the same thing over and over again?

15._____Does it ever seem to you that no one wants you to have what you want?

16._____Do you ever tell stories of not getting what you asked for?

17._____Do you ever say, "I want you to offer it," and when your partner does, you say your partner offered it only because you asked for it?

18._____Do you ever feel uncomfortable when another person is getting all the attention?

19._____Do you ever feel like "nothing is good enough"?

20._____Do you ever feel uncomfortable wanting things for yourself?

21._____Do you ever feel uncomfortable with your desires?

22._____Do you say you don't want it and then complain about not getting it?

23._____Do you see everyone else as having what he or she wants?

24._____Do you envy other people having good things you don't have?

25._____Do you ever have trouble accepting others' positive valuations of you—your worth, ability?

26._____Do you ever see someone else receive something you don't feel he or she deserves?

27._____Do you ever feel uncomfortable giving something to yourself?

28._____Do you ever feel critical of someone who whines?

29._____Do you ever feel critical of someone who is needy?

30._____Do you ever feel like a bad person?

31._____Do you ever feel worthless?

32._____Do you ever feel like a failure?

33._____Do you ever feel depressed?

34._____Do you feel chronic anger at others who are fortunate?

35._____Do you ever feel like you put forth a false "good" self and hide your true "bad" self?

36._____Do you ever have trouble imagining why others like and accept praise?

37._____Do you ever feel critical of people who ask for reassurance?

38._____Do you ever feel uncomfortable with people who want nurturing?

39._____Do you feel uncomfortable when other people ask for things from you?

40.＿＿Do you ever feel like you have nothing to give?

41.＿＿Do you ever think that if you take what you ask for, you can't ask for anything else?

42.＿＿Do you ever feel that if you get what you want, you can't complain anymore?

43.＿＿Do you get jealous of those who have what they want?

44.＿＿Do you ever feel you have been destined by fate to suffer deprivation?

45.＿＿Do you feel deprived by fate of your blessings?

46.＿＿Do you ever get a compliment and think, *If you knew what I was really like, you would not say that*?

47.＿＿Do you ever feel useless?

48.＿＿Do you ever get gifts and then give them away?

49.＿＿Do you ever feel uncomfortable asking for nurturing?

50.＿＿Do you ever get what you ask for and then feel empty?

STEP 2.

Each item on the list is worth one point for a total of 50 points. To calculate your "positive receiving quotient," count the items marked N. To calculate your "negative receiving quotient," count the total items marked S and O. If your N number is greater than your S and O number, then your "positive receiving quotient" is higher than your "negative receiving quotient." That is, you generally find it easier to accept gifts than to turn them away, and to witness others receiving gifts, rather than ignoring the event. If your S and O number is higher than your N number, then you have a higher "negative receiving quotient" and being receptive to gifts and witnessing others receiving gifts is a major challenge for you.

STEP 3.

Look at all the statements you marked S and O from the perspective of a separate knower. This will help you see the facts of your behavior. Then, look at the same statements from the perspective of a connected knower. Call into play your emotions and intuitions. Allow yourself to experience yourself as someone who gives. Connect to that part of yourself with appreciation.

STEP 4.

Finally, look at all the statements you marked with an N. Simply notice where you're having trouble with giving and think about how you can change yourself to a person who finds it easier to give.

STEP 5.

Ask your partner to complete Steps 1, 2, 3, and 4.

STEP 6.

Ask your partner for an Imago Dialogue for the purpose of sharing your discoveries with each other.

Be sure to note items on your partner's list that are the same as or different from yours. You may find that you have answered differently in many instances. One of you is probably more open to receiving in a particular situation, and one of you is probably more resistant. Next, look at all the items marked S and O on *both* of your lists, and think about how each of you might open your heart to be even more receptive. One way you can facilitate your growth is to take each item that you marked with an S or an O and change it to a positive statement.

EXAMPLE:

After Karen and Karl did this exercise, they had an Imago Dialogue about how they had each answered the questions. In sharing their responses, they learned some things that surprised them.

Karen told Karl how she answered question #42: "This question made me realize that if I complained about something you did and then you stopped doing it, I thought I had no right to complain about anything else. I remember when I asked you to please put your dirty clothes in the hamper, and then when you started doing that, I bit my tongue over the fact that you never loaded the dishwasher, which bothered me just as much." Karl was surprised that his wife felt she was restricted in this way. His response was, "Why don't you just tell me what's bothering you? That's better than having you be upset and me not having a clue why."

On the other hand, Karen was surprised to hear her husband talk about how often he felt he had to hide his "bad" self with a "good guy" front (question #35). He told her, "I'm just now becoming aware of how often I hide, even in front of you. I'm embarrassed to say it, but I guess I'm afraid you won't love me if you know how flawed I am." Karen's response was humorous, but loving: "I have news for you, honey. I already know you're not perfect! But I would like to know more of the real you."

This exercise gave Karen and Karl a deeper appreciation for how different they were as individuals, yet how connected they were by both having wounded places, even if those places were different. They learned more about each other's tender spots and were more empathic with each other's struggles to grow beyond their limitations.

Karen was able to change #42 into a positive statement for herself: "I believe I have the right to voice a particular dissatisfaction, even in the face of having been given something I really want in another unrelated area of my life."

Although it took time and continued support from Karen, Karl was gradually able to change #35 by saying, "I no longer have to hide part of myself with a more acceptable façade, because I no longer believe that the part I was hiding was 'bad.'" Through the repeated experience of having his honest feelings accepted by Karen over time, Karl retrained himself to believe that he was as he was, and that was okay with the person who loved him the most.

Until you have a clear picture of the attitudes and beliefs that fuel your behaviors, you can't change them.

This exercise will give you and your partner information about yourselves and each other that you have not had before. It gives you the opportunity to turn your difficulties with self-esteem and receiving love around so that current difficulties can become future strengths.

BETWEEN-SESSION ASSIGNMENTS

- At least once each week, look at the statements you answered with an S for sometimes or an O for often. Ask your partner for an Imago Dialogue where you talk about why it has been hard for you to receive or witness these gifts, and how you want to become more open to them.

- Then, have an Imago Dialogue where you are the Receiver and your partner is the Sender. Mirror, validate, and empathize with your partner's experiences of difficulty in accepting or witnessing certain gifts, and how he or she wants to become more open to them.

- Use what you have been learning from previous sessions to have an Imago Dialogue with your partner that is centered around asking for a gift. Follow the instructions for the exercise in Session 4, page 56, titled, "Practice Asking for and Receiving a Gift, *and* Giving a Gift. "To make this dialogue even more integrated, make it so the gift you ask for is from the Dream Gift List your partner has been keep for you (as described in the exercise on page 22 in Session 1). Practice it, with you and your partner each taking a turn being the Receiver.

Your "Giving Love" Assessment

REVIEW IN *RECEIVING LOVE*

Chapter 1, "The Pattern," pages 27–30

TIME FRAME

30 minutes

SPECIAL CONSIDERATIONS

This session is the mirror image of Session 6. You will be completing a detailed questionnaire that allows you to examine your attitudes and behaviors about giving gifts. Allow yourself the time and emotional space to consider the questions carefully.

WHAT YOU NEED TO KNOW

This session will help you uncover patterns in your giving behavior that you may not have been aware of before. Sharing your answers with your partner will provide you with information about how your individual patterns of giving and receiving fit together in the kinds of relationship interactions you have currently established.

EXERCISE

Examining How Giving You Are

Time: 30 minutes

OBJECTIVE

- To understand and begin to improve your ability to give gifts, praise, and love.

STEP 1.

Below are 50 question designed to help you discover what we are calling your "giving quotient." Answer how often you do what is stated by marking each item with S for "sometimes," O for "often," or N for "never" or "rarely." The number of Ss and Os will measure your "positive giving quotient." The number of Ns will measure your "negative giving quotient."

As was true when assessing your "receiving quotient," allow yourself to consider your answers from both a separate and connected knowing perspective. Consider each statement from the point of view that examines the facts of your behavior, *and* the emotional point of view that considers your feelings.

1. _____ I feel comfortable bragging about someone.

2. _____ I feel positive when someone brags about himself or herself.

3. _____ I feel positive toward someone else who is bragged about by another person.

4. _____ I give gifts without expecting others to feel obligated.

5. _____ I give gifts and do not remember I gave them.

6. _____ I give gifts to people who value them.

7. _____ I accept people who refuse to take my gifts.

8. _____ I give compliments to others easily.

9. _____ I express love easily and freely.

10. _____ I tend to remember only the good times.

11. _____ When I give a gift, I do not expect to be thanked.

12. _____ I express appreciation for the gifts other people give me.

13. _____ I try to give gifts that other people say they want.

14. _____ I give without telling stories about my giving.

15. _____ I like giving anonymous gifts.

16. _____ I feel comfortable when another person is getting all the attention.

17. _____ I give to needy people.

18. _____ I feel comfortable giving to myself.

19.____I have a desire to give.

20.____I give without complaining.

21.____I like seeing other people have what they want.

22.____I share the joy of other people who have good things I don't have.

23.____I positively affirm the value of other people—their worth, their ability.

24.____I feel full inside when I give.

25.____I feel comfortable when other people give things to themselves.

26.____I believe giving expands me.

27.____I feel loving toward people who are needy.

28.____I feel like I am a good person.

29.____I value myself.

30.____I feel like a success.

31.____I feel happy most of the time.

32.____I celebrate the good fortune of other people.

33.____I try to show my best self at all times.

34.____I support others who like and want praise.

35.____I willingly reassure others who need it or ask for it.

36.____I feel comfortable nurturing others.

37.____I feel comfortable when others ask me for something.

38.____I feel like I have a lot to give.

39.____I feel a lot of joy when I give.

40.____I give full attention to people who complain.

41.____I love it when other people get what they want.

42.____I give full attention to people when they are talking to me.

43.____I give praise to God or to fate for my blessings.

44._____I give myself good health care.

45._____I like it when someone lets him or herself be bragged about.

46._____I always feel valuable and useful.

47._____I feel blessed to be able to give.

48._____I give gifts to persons whom I don't like.

49._____I am glad to be alive.

50._____I praise God for the gift of life.

STEP 2.

Each item on the list is worth one point for a total of 50 points. To calculate your "positive giving quotient," which is your ability to give, count the total items marked S and O. To calculate your "negative giving quotient," or the difficulty you have with giving, count the items marked N. If your N number is greater than your S and O number, then your "negative giving quotient" is higher than your "positive giving quotient." If your S and O number is higher than your N number, then you have a higher "positive giving quotient."

STEP 3.

Look at all the statements you marked S or O from the perspective of a separate knower. This will help you see the facts of your giving behavior. Then, look at the same statements from the perspective of a connected knower. Call into play your emotions and intuitions. Allow yourself to experience yourself as someone who gives. Connect to that part of yourself with appreciation.

STEP 4.

Finally, look at all the statements you marked with an N. Simply notice where you're having trouble with giving and think about how you can change yourself to a person who finds it easier to give.

STEP 5.

Ask your partner to complete Steps 1, 2, 3, and 4.

STEP 6.

Ask your partner for an Imago Dialogue for the purpose of sharing your discoveries with each other.

Be sure to note items on your partner's list that are the same as or different from yours. You may find that you have answered differently in many instances. One of you is probably more open to giving in a particular situation, and one of you is probably more resistant. Next, look at all the items marked S and O on *both* of your lists, and think about how each of you might open your heart to be even more giving. One way you can facilitate your growth is to take each item that you marked with an S or an O and change it into a positive statement.

As you and your partner review your scores on this questionnaire, think of your "negative giving quotient" as an opportunity for growth, and not as in indictment of your character. You can change it. You *can* make a commitment to help each other open your hearts to all the ways of giving that are represented on this list. No matter how many Ns you had on your questionnaire today, you can have all Ss and Os at some point in the future.

EXAMPLE:

Karen was distressed to see how much trouble she had being happy when others were praised and praising other people (questions 32, 34, and 35). In fact, she told Karl she was horrified by how ungenerous she was in this way. To help herself begin to change, she intentionally went through the 50 questions again and answered them as though she were absolutely generous with her delight at other people's good fortune. She had to change several of her Ns to Os. In that way, she could rehearse in her mind and imagination the behavior she wanted to see herself manifest in her real life.

Karl learned that he was only too ready to give to others, but had trouble giving to himself (question #18). Although he didn't want to stop being generous, he decided that he did want to work on being more generous to himself. He asked for Karen's help in pointing out to him when she noticed that he was short-changing his own needs and desires in favor of pleasing others.

BETWEEN-SESSION ASSIGNMENTS

- At least once this week, have an Imago Dialogue with your partner about one gift you were able to give. As the Sender, share how it felt to offer the gift. Then, let your partner be the Sender and tell you how it felt to give you a gift. Be sure that the Receiver mirrors, validates, and empathizes every time a message is sent.
- Offer to give your partner a gift from the Dream Gift List (Session 1, page 22) that you have been keeping for him or her. Tell your partner why you have chosen that particular gift. Explain this to your partner from both a separate and connected knowing

point of view (Session 2, page 37). An example of separate knowing would be, "I chose this gift because you said you wanted it." An example of connected knowing would be, "I just felt that this is something you would enjoy." Engage in an Imago Dialogue, with you as the Sender talking about your experience as the giver. Remember that the concept of giving a gift includes being able to witness someone else getting something without feeling jealous or bad about yourself.

Your Imago

REVIEW IN *RECEIVING LOVE*

TIME FRAME

Approximately 1 hour for each part for a total of 3 hours

SPECIAL CONSIDERATIONS

There is a lot of material in this session. You may want to complete the exercises in one long session, or you may find that it works better for you to do one part at a time for a total of three sessions this week.

WHAT YOU NEED TO KNOW

Our ability to receive and to give is greatly influenced by the relationship we had with our caretakers when we were children. We have absorbed their patterns of giving and receiving without realizing it, and we continue to live those patterns out in our significant adult relationships.

In addition to the *covert* messages our caretakers gave us through the behavior they modeled, they also sent us *overt* messages about giving and receiving. They coached us on when and what we could accept, what we could not accept, and when, what, and in what ways it was appropriate for us to give. They verbalized whatever their "rules" of giving and receiving happened to be.

In response to these two sets of messages, we made a series of conscious and unconscious decisions that played into the formation of our identity as individuals. These parental messages about giving and receiving are densely woven in to the answers we give to basic questions, such as: "Who am I?" "What do I deserve?" "What can I expect from my life?" "What can I expect from my intimate relationships?"

It isn't possible to answer questions such as these without uncovering our attitudes and behaviors regarding giving and receiving. Since decisions about giving and receiving are not always made consciously, we can only get a complete picture of what they are by looking at our current thoughts, feelings, words, and behaviors. That is, we must increase our level of self-awareness.

People enter relationships with varying degrees of self-awareness. Everyone is aware to some extent of the important people and events that have made them who they are. But most of us do not know the extent to which we continue to be influenced by our previous experiences. We are formed from every important relationship we've ever had. Take a look at any marriage, and you will find ghosts from each partner's past. Mothers, fathers, former lovers, best friends, coaches, and special teachers occupy every marriage and influence the way individuals become partners.

Central to Imago Relationship Therapy is the concept of the imago, a Latin term meaning "image." Your imago is the unconscious picture you have in your brain of all the people who influenced you most strongly at an early age. Most often, your imago is composed from experiences you've had with the parent you had the most conflict or difficulty with as a child. Without knowing it, all of us scan potential partners looking for an imago match, someone who has the same characteristics as our most problematic parent. This person offers us the chance to replay those early conflicts, and the possibility of healing them in a way we cannot with our parents. So, Joanie, who had an overbearing father, is attracted to Jeff, who is domineering and authoritarian. Jeff, whose mother was self-abnegating and anxious to please, is attracted to Joanie, who is nurturing and looking for a strong man to guide her. They are an imago match. Neither of them recognizes the unconscious forces that have attracted them to each other. They are in for struggle in their marriage, and they also have the potential for healing, through their relationship with each other, the wounds they were dealt as children.

This session will help you unearth the important influences from your childhood that are part of your imago. This section is designed to help you get a better idea of where your ideas about giving and receiving come from and how they are manifested in your life today. There are three parts: Part I helps you clarify your parents' messages about giving and receiving; Part II helps you clarify your partner's messages about giving and receiving; Part III helps you and your partner identify the messages about giving and receiving that you want to hear and act on. When you and your partner have completed this session, you will be aware of the role that your attitudes toward giving and receiving play in your life, and how they affect you as a couple.

PART I: Influences from Childhood

EXERCISE

What I Got from My Parents or
Other Caretakers

Time: 1 hour

OBJECTIVES

- To understand what childhood messages about giving and receiving influenced you.

- To understand how those messages influence you in your relationship today.

STEP 1.

On the chart below, or on a separate sheet of paper, make a list of positive and negative traits that describe your parents or other significant caretakers, as you recall them.

MOTHER		FATHER	
Positive Traits	Negative Traits	Positive Traits	Negative Traits

EXAMPLE:

Wendy filled out the chart this way.

MOTHER		FATHER	
Positive Traits	Negative Traits	Positive Traits	Negative Traits
—intelligent —creative —independent —adventurous	—emotionally cold —easily offended —ambitious for her children	—intelligent —strong moral sense —socially adept	—alcoholic —short-tempered —judgmental —sexist

STEP 2.

Read through the list below and think about which of these attributes was acceptable to want in your family. Which were valued and sanctioned as allowable objects of desire? For simplicity's sake, circle the ones that were acceptable regardless of whether the okay came from your mother, your father, or other caretakers. The adult figures in your life probably had quite different ideas about what was okay and what wasn't, but all we want to do now is get a clearer idea of what messages *you* got in childhood, whatever the source.

In my family it was okay to want: love, sex, play, fun, intelligence, body touch, nurturing, rest, movement, feelings, sleep, education, work, success, happiness, health, food, vacations, spirituality, religious beliefs, touch, laughter, support, warmth, praise, knowledge, your own thoughts, sympathy for others, money, property, recreation, freedom, independence, compliments, negative feelings, hope, orgasms, massages, fear, sadness, anger, grief, joy, peace, equality, pleasure, musical talent, creativity, artistic talent, faith, doubt, desires, athletic talent, competition, trust, fatigue, respect, tolerance, appreciation, gratitude, empathy (add any other words that you wish).

EXAMPLE:

When Wendy responded to the question in Step 2, she found that in her family it was okay to want: play, fun, intelligence, rest, education, happiness, food, praise, sympathy for others, money, hope, joy, pleasure, musical talent, artistic talent, and appreciation.

Now, read through the list again and draw a single line through the attributes that it was **not** okay to want in your family.

*In my family it was **not okay** to want:* love, sex, play, fun, intelligence, body touch, nurturing, rest, movement, feelings, sleep, education, work, success, happiness, health, food, vacations, spirituality, religious beliefs, touch, laughter, support, warmth, praise, knowledge, your own thoughts, sympathy for others, money, property, recreation, freedom, independence, compliments, negative feelings, hope, orgasms, massages, fear, sadness, anger, grief, joy, peace, equality, pleasure, musical talent, creativity, artistic talent, faith, doubt, desires, athletic talent, competition, trust, fatigue, respect, tolerance, appreciation, gratitude, empathy (add any other words that you wish).

EXAMPLE:

*Here is Wendy's list for what was **not** okay to want in her family: nurturing, feelings, religious beliefs, negative feelings, anger, grief, faith, desires, and competition.*

STEP 3.

Use the chart below to list what was okay to want, and **not** okay to want, in your family.

It was okay to want: It was **not** okay to want:

_____   _____

_____   _____

_____   _____

_____   _____

STEP 4.

Identifying what was okay to want in your family will help you see what was acceptable to receive and to give. Answering the questions below will take some time and thought. There isn't necessarily a linear relationship between wanting, receiving, and giving. For example, in some instances, you might feel that it's okay to give a particular thing, but not okay to receive it yourself.

Refer back to the list you made in Step 3. As you consider each attribute on your positive and negative lists, ask yourself whether it was okay or **not** okay to receive and give each one. Then fill in the following statements about receiving and giving.

In my family, it was okay to expect to receive, or to receive: _____

_____

_____

_____

In my family it was **not** okay to expect to receive, or to receive: _____

_____

_____

_____

In my family it was okay to expect to give, or to give: _____

_____

_____

_____

In my family it was **not** okay to expect to give, or to give: _____

_____

_____

_____

EXAMPLE:

This is how Wendy answered the questions in Step 4.

In Wendy's family, it was okay to expect to receive, or to receive: handmade gifts, compliments for competence, and praise for good behavior.

*In Wendy's family it was **not** okay to expect to receive, or to receive: emotional coddling, the expression of strong feelings, non-judgmental support, extravagant gifts, monetary gifts, or loans from family members.*

In Wendy's family it was okay to expect to give, or to give: inexpensive gifts that were appropriate to your financial situation, emotional support that observed an English sense of privacy and decorum, gifts that had a utilitarian purpose, and humor instead of heartfelt feeling.

*In Wendy's family it was **not** okay to expect to give, or to give: the shirt off your back, sharing your home or your bank account, or sharing private experiences and information even if it would be helpful.*

STEP 5.

You have just identified some of the central messages you received from your parents, or other caretakers, about what you could give and what you could receive. Now take this information a step further and write down what consequences were attached to obeying or disobeying these negative and positive messages.

If I obeyed the negative messages, then: _____

_____

_____

_____

If I **disobeyed** the negative messages, then: _____

_____

_____

_____

If I obeyed the positive messages, then: _____

_____

_____

_____

If I **disobeyed** the positive messages, then: _____

_____

_____

_____

EXAMPLE:

Wendy filled out the above form as follows.

If I obeyed the negative messages, then: I would stay safe. My parents would like me. I would be a good person.

*If I **disobeyed** the negative messages, then: I would be selfish. I would be socially embarrassing. I wouldn't be a good person.*

If I obeyed the positive messages, then: I would be happy. I would be successful.

*If I **disobeyed** the positive messages, then: I wouldn't find a husband or have children. I would be a failure. I would be a disappointment to my parents.*

STEP 6.

From these general statements, use the following form to write down which messages you obeyed, which you disobeyed, and what the consequences were.

The negative messages I obeyed were _____

_____

_____

and the consequences were _____

_____

_____

_____

The negative messages I **disobeyed** were _____

_____

_____

_____

and the consequences were _____

_____

_____

_____

The positive messages I obeyed were _____

_____

_____

_____

and the consequences were _____

_____

_____

_____

The positive messages I **disobeyed** were _____

_____

_____

_____

and the consequences were _____

_____

_____

_____

EXAMPLE:

Wendy answered the questions in Step 6 this way.

The negative messages Wendy obeyed were: She did not express her feelings openly to very many people. She did not show her anger. She tried to stay away from situations where she would have to compete.

And the consequences were: She was perceived as standoffish by her friends. She put up with behavior from others that she wouldn't have if she had recognized that she was angry and had a right to be angry. She had trouble owning her gifts and abilities, because she tried to stay away from competitive situations, and when she did do something well, she couldn't claim it in case someone else felt bad as a result.

*The negative messages Wendy **disobeyed** were: She allowed herself to develop a religious faith. She gave herself permission to want things.*

And the consequences were: Her religious faith gave her great comfort and allowed her to grow as a person. She learned to ignore her family's cynicism. She had to practice recognizing and saying what she wanted, but eventually got to the point where she could do it with a minimum of struggle.

The positive messages Wendy obeyed were: She got herself a good education. She was compassionate. She felt it was okay for her to be successful.

And the consequences were: Knowing that she had earned a good education gave her self-confidence. Her world was enriched by the feelings of compassion she had for others, and her relationships were good as a result. She felt fine about her level of professional success.

*The positive messages Wendy **disobeyed** were: She didn't develop her creative side. She didn't focus on making money.*

And the consequences were: There were a lot of arts and crafts she was attracted to, but she didn't feel like she would ever be able to do them. She didn't have as much financial security as she would like, and that caused her some worry.

STEP 7.

Now, given the messages you obeyed, what decisions did you make about:

Who I am: _____

_____

_____

_____

What I descrve: _____

_____

_____

_____

What I don't deserve: _____

_____

_____

_____

Given who I am, what I deserve, and what I don't deserve, I can expect from life that:

_____

_____

_____

These expectations have had an impact on what kind of partner I have chosen and what I can expect from my intimate relationship. From my intimate relationship, I can expect:

_____

_____

_____

EXAMPLE:

Wendy answered the questions in Step 7 this way.

Who I am: I feel that I am a successful person most of the time. I have a lot of friends and try to help others whenever I can. My compassion has made me a better mother.

What I deserve: I am a good person, but I don't deserve more than anyone else.

What I don't deserve: I don't deserve to be treated badly. Neither do I deserve more of the good things in life than anybody else.

I can expect from life that: I will achieve medium happiness and a moderate amount of success. From my intimate relationship, I can expect: I hope that my partner and I will get along fine. I don't have to be ecstatic, as long as the relationship doesn't have a lot of conflict. I expect to be able to maintain some privacy and to treat each other with respect, if not always with passion.

STEP 8.

You can get a clearer understanding of how your childhood messages have carried forward into your current life by answering the following questions.

Which messages are you still obeying? _____

_____

_____

What consequences are you still experiencing? _____

_____

_____

EXAMPLE:

Here are the answers Wendy gave to the questions in Step 8.

She is still obeying the message not to be competitive. As a result, she has trouble setting goals for herself and going after what she wants.

STEP 9.

Finally, let's look at which of these early childhood messages are no longer serving you well.

Which early messages do you want to change? _____

_____

_____

_____

_____

Instead of these old messages, what new messages do you want to guide your life? _____

_____

_____

_____

What will you have to change about yourself to negate the old messages and instill the new ones? _____

_____

_____

_____

EXAMPLE:

Wendy answered the questions in Step 9 like this.

Which early messages do I want to change? I want to have all my feelings be acceptable. I want it to be okay for me to have needs. I want it to be okay for me to be successful.

What new messages do I want to guide my life? That it's okay for me to feel whatever I feel without being ashamed or feeling diminished. That every human being has vulnerabilities and needs, and it isn't a sign of weakness to express them. That it's okay for me to achieve more success than other members of my family.

What will I have to change about myself to negate the old messages and instill the new ones? In recent years, I've made an attempt to share more of myself with friends, my sisters, and my husband. I want to continue stretching beyond my comfort level so I can feel that other people care about this deeper part of me, and that they can be trusted. I also have to stay aware of whenever I start sabotaging my own success.

STEP 10.

Using what you have learned about the Imago Dialogue from Session 2, and the weekly practice sessions you have been engaged in during the course of following this workbook, ask your partner to have an Imago Dialogue with you about Part I.

Although you could have a dialogue about any of the previous 9 steps, we suggest you begin with Step 9. Offer to be the Sender and share with your partner how you answered the three questions in Step 9: what early messages you want to change; what new messages you want to guide your life; and what you will have to change about yourself to negate the old messages and instill the new ones. Here's how you might begin.

- The Sender would refer back to data he or she filled out in the particular step.
- The Receiver would listen and then mirror.
- The Receiver would check to see if the mirror was accurate.
- If it was accurate, the Receiver would ask if there was more the Sender wanted to say about that.
- If not, the Receiver then would validate the Sender's words and feelings.
- Next, the Receiver would empathize with the Sender.
- At this point, the two partners can exchange roles, or the original Sender can continue by talking about his or her father, using the process described above. After the original Sender has talked about his or her father, switch places.

Imago Dialogue will allow you to get the greatest benefit from having done all this work, since you will both be sharing the essence of what you've learned about the early influences in your life.

PART II: Current Influences

Using a similar process as that in Part I, you will discover the messages your partner received from his or her caretakers about giving and receiving, and the messages he or she sends to you about receiving and giving.

<u>EXERCISE</u>

The Beliefs My Partner Brought to Our Relationship

Time: 1 hour

OBJECTIVE

- To gain insight into the imago of your partner, so that you will be able to make this information a conscious part of your interactions.

STEP 1.

Your caretakers aren't the only source of messages about which attitudes and beliefs toward giving and receiving are acceptable and which aren't. You have probably been influenced by former partners, teachers, coaches, friends, bosses, and coworkers, just to name a few. Of these, though, your current partner is probably the most influential. Since this exercise asks you for your opinion about which messages he or she sends you, it is entirely subjective. It could be that in some instances, *you think* your partner holds a particular belief, but you are wrong. Your own projection has colored your assessment. Nevertheless, based on our years of experience working with couples, we predict that your responses will be accurate most of the time.

Using the same list of attributes we used in Part I, circle the ones that are okay to want according to your partner.

My partner has let me know it's okay to want: love, sex, play, fun, intelligence, body touch, nurturing, rest, movement, feelings, sleep, education, work, success, happiness, health, food, vacations, spirituality, religious beliefs, touch, laughter, support, warmth, praise, knowledge, your own thoughts, sympathy for others, money, property, recreation, freedom, independence, compliments, negative feelings, hope, orgasms, massages, fear, sadness, anger, grief, joy, peace, equality, pleasure, musical talent, creativity, artistic talent, faith, doubt, desires, athletic talent, competition, trust, belief, fatigue, respect, tolerance, appreciation, gratitude, empathy (add any other words that you wish).

Now, review the list again and draw a single a line through those things that are **not** okay to want according to your partner.

*My partner has let me know it's **not** okay to want:* love, sex, play, fun, intelligence, body touch, nurturing, rest, movement, feelings, sleep, education, work, success, happiness, health, food, vacations, spirituality, religious beliefs, touch, laughter, support, warmth, praise, knowledge, your own thoughts, sympathy for others, money, property, recreation, freedom, independence, compliments, negative feelings, hope, orgasms, massages, fear, sadness, anger, grief, joy, peace, equality, pleasure, musical talent, creativity, artistic talent, faith, doubt, desires, athletic talent, competition, trust, belief, fatigue, respect, tolerance, appreciation, gratitude, empathy (add any other words that you wish).

STEP 2.

Use the chart below to list what your partner thinks is okay to want and **not** okay to want.

It is okay to want: It is **not** okay to want:

_____   _____

_____   _____

_____   _____

_____   _____

STEP 3.

Based upon the lists you compiled in Step 2, complete the sentences below with messages *you think* your partner received from his or her caretakers.

My partner feels it's okay to expect to receive, or to receive: _____

_____

_____

_____

My partner feels it's **not** okay to expect to receive, or to receive: _____

_____

_____

_____

My partner feels it's okay to expect to give, or to give: _____

_____

_____

_____

My partner feels it's **not** okay to expect to give, or to give: _____

_____

_____

_____

EXAMPLE:

Wendy answered the questions about her husband this way.

My husband feels it's okay to receive physical affection, praise, presents that reflect his interests, and special meals that I make for him.

*My husband feels it's **not** okay to receive expensive presents, public displays of affection, appreciation for his looks.*

My husband feels it's okay to give me small treats from the grocery store, compliments to me about the way I look, compliments about my social skills, and to give practical presents to the kids.

*My husband feels it's **not** okay to give gifts that he considers to be luxuries, gifts that he thinks are silly, shallow, or frivolous.*

STEP 4.

Review the lists you compiled in Step 2 again, and this time, complete the sentences with messages *your partner sends to you.*

In my relationship with my partner, it's okay for me to expect to receive, or to receive:

_____

_____

_____

In my relationship with my partner, it's **not** okay for me to expect to receive, or to receive:

_____

_____

_____

In my relationship with my partner, it's okay for me to expect to give, or to give:

_____

_____

_____

In my relationship with my partner, it's **not** okay for me to expect to give, or to give:

_____

_____

_____

These messages indicate what prohibitions and permissions around receiving and giving exist in your relationship.

EXAMPLE:

Wendy answered the questions above in this way.

In my relationship with my partner, it's okay for me to receive: Appreciation he voluntarily gives on his own. Compliments about how I look. Presents he gives me on special occasions.

*In my relationship with my partner, it's **not** okay for me to receive: Praise and appreciation I have to ask for. Expensive or elaborate presents that are outside our budget.*

In my relationship with my partner, it's okay for me to give: Specific praise or appreciation for particular things he's done. Enthusiastic interest in sex.

*In my relationship with my partner, it's **not** okay for me to give: General appreciation for what a good person he is. Too much appreciation for other men. Too much support to my friends.*

STEP 5.

Engage your partner in an Imago Dialogue about what you each learned from completing Part II by sharing your answers to Step 4. Because there is emotional content to the information you will be sharing, be certain to follow the process of having the Receiver mirror, validate, and empathize. This is not the time to disagree or challenge what the Sender is saying. The task here is to receive fully the Sender's *perceptions* of the attitudes and beliefs the other partner has brought to the relationship.

You and your partner will no doubt have different perspectives on some of these points. Engaging in an Imago Dialogue will help you both clarify where your perspectives are distinct, and where they are similar. Take your time to understand how each of you perceives the messages you are giving to each other about giving and receiving. Here's how you might begin.

- The Sender would refer back to data he or she filled out in the particular step.
- The Receiver would listen and then mirror.
- The Receiver would check to see if the mirror was accurate.
- If it was accurate, the Receiver would ask if there was more the Sender wanted to say about that.
- If not, the Receiver then would validate the Sender's words and feelings.
- Next, the Receiver would empathize with the Sender.
- At this point, the two partners can exchange roles, or the original Sender can continue by talking about his or her father, using the process described above. After the original Sender has talked about his or her father, switch places.

PART III: Choosing the Messages of the Future

Deciding How I Want to Give and Receive Now

Time: 1 hour

OBJECTIVE

• To choose the messages you want to give and receive in the future.

STEP 1.

Write down the messages you wish you had heard from your mother, father, or other significant caretakers; the messages you want to hear from your partner; and the new permissions you will give to yourself for giving and receiving.

I wish I had heard these messages about giving and receiving from my mother:

_____

_____

_____

I wish I had heard these messages about giving and receiving from my father:

_____

_____

_____

I want to hear these messages about giving and receiving from my partner:

_____

_____

_____

I now give myself permission to give and receive in these new ways:

_____

_____

_____

EXAMPLE:

Wendy wished her mother had told her it was okay to work hard in a career and be successful. She wished her father had told her she was attractive as a woman. From her husband, she wanted to hear that he understood why she wanted to indulge herself with the occasional luxury, and that giving each other gifts for their garden would enrich their lives. She was ready to give herself permission to acknowledge her desire for things that were beyond practical necessities, that fed her love of richness and color and beauty.

STEP 2.

Using Imago Dialogue, have your partner share his or her responses to the questions in Step 1. Then, switch roles so that you are the Sender and your partner is the Receiver. By completing this Imago Dialogue, you will learn where your barriers to giving and receiving come from, and you will be able to identify the areas the two of you want to work on in the future. Be sure to mirror, validate, and empathize. Also, when your partner shares with you whatever he or she is ready to receive, you can add that item to the Dream Gift List you are keeping for your partner from Session 1 (see page 22).

BETWEEN-SESSION ASSIGNMENTS

Some couples would do well to have a separate Imago Dialogue for each step of each exercise in this session. That means, for example, that your first dialogue would center on Step 1 of the first exercise, "What I Got from My Parents or Other Caretakers" (see page 79), where you assigned positive and negative qualities to your mother and father, or other caretakers. Here's how you might begin.

- The Sender would refer back to data he or she filled out in the particular step.
- The Receiver would listen and then mirror.
- The Receiver would check to see if the mirror was accurate.
- If it was accurate, the Receiver would ask if there was more the Sender wanted to say about that.

- If not, the Receiver then would validate the Sender's words and feelings.
- Next, the Receiver would empathize with the Sender.
- At this point, the two partners can exchange roles, or the original Sender can continue by talking about his or her father, using the process described above. After the original Sender has talked about his or her father, switch places.

The next dialogue would be scheduled for a different time and place. It would center on Step 2 on page 80, which identifies what was okay and not okay to want in your family.

At least once a week, sit down with your partner and talk about how, in Part III, you concluded the sentence stem, "I now give myself permission to give and receive in these new ways." This is a good subject for an Imago Dialogue. Tell your partner whether you have found opportunities to expand your capacity for giving and receiving in the ways you indicated when answering this question, and whether you were able to take advantage of those opportunities. Then invite your partner to share the ways he or she has found to become a better giver and receiver. Because this Session is intensive, focus on using Imago Dialogue for the purpose of understanding the material presented here, instead of also trying to review past material.

Barriers to Intimacy

REVIEW IN *RECEIVING LOVE*

Chapter 3, "Tuning In," pages 53–54

Chapter 4, "The Present Is a Window into the Past," pages 73–74, and "Splitting," pages 74–82

Chapter 5, "Connecting the Dots," pages 104–106

TIME FRAME

Approximately 30 minutes for each exercise, for a total of 1 hour and 30 minutes

SPECIAL CONSIDERATIONS

At first glance, this session can look complex. But you will be able to follow a single theme in your life back to wounds you received in particular stages of your childhood development. Being able to identify these problems will lead directly to actions you can take today to heal the wound and redirect your attitudes and behaviors to ones that improve your primary relationship.

WHAT YOU NEED TO KNOW

Many of us are afraid of our desire to be loved, or we get anxious when love is offered to us. Our fears, rooted in childhood wounds, show up as barriers to intimacy that interfere with our ability to receive and give love. Identifying these fears, honoring them, and developing a plan with our partner for mutual healing is the way through the barriers caused by these fears.

Any couple can create a conscious partnership if the motivation to do so is strong enough. The first step toward conscious partnership is to understand how the child is the father of the man. How have our earlier experiences affected our functioning as adults? The particular ways we were supported or not supported through the established developmental stages of childhood is formative. Parents are our first great moral teachers. We know that children want to please their parents and be just like them.

Every stage of development has its challenges for the child, who learns how to master new skills through his parents' guidance. The child ventures out and tries something new and then returns to the safety and support of his parents. His development depends on a rhythm that propels him forward, even as he comes back around to revisit previous tasks. This rhythm is not just an oscillation, but also a progression. Each time he returns to his primary connection with his caretaker, he responds to another developmental impulse that pushes him toward the next stage of growth. It is as if the child were being blown unerringly toward the gates of maturity by the wise breath of nature. Through one transformation after another his life flows until he arrives at adulthood.

The developmental stages exist because inside each child there is an impulse to do what will best help that child become an adult. This inner drive for survival and completion impels every child to become attached, to separate, to explore and differentiate, to develop an identity of his or her own, to achieve competence, to develop social concern for others, and, finally, to achieve intimacy with another person, so that the transition to adulthood can be completed. It is part of nature's plan to move the child safely and quickly through these vulnerable young years. Nature is interested in producing adults who have successfully completed the developmental tasks through well-defined stages that will equip them to continue the survival of the species.

Each of these stages has it own challenge and its own opportunity. A particular impulse comes into focus around a particular age for the first time. If the impulse is supported and its aim is accomplished successfully, the child is able to integrate the increasing mental, emotional, and physical complexity. A good foundation has been laid for learning the next lesson and for mastering the original impulse at an increasing level of complexity when it shows up later in a different form.

If the child remains secure in his connection to his primary caretaker, he will then become interested in exploring his environment. If that is a success, he will identify with certain objects or persons and integrate them into a personal identity, and so on. There is no guarantee, but there is an increased probability that all will be well if each impulse is successfully integrated when it first appears as an internal imperative. Think of a spiral staircase where each step is a progression upward in space, but is also a repetition of a particular point around the circumference of the circle. We spend our lives walking up our own spiral staircases. At each turn, we get the same view we had before at the same spot, but because we are higher up, the view is broader.

At some point, however, we inevitably stumble and fall on a particular step. Although we keep on walking upward, we leave behind a trail that testifies to our injury. Looking back, we can trace the trail to its source and see how our misstep has affected our own successive stages of growth and our ability to help other people, especially our children, negotiate this same step on their own personal journeys.

There are many reasons why we may not be able to plant our feet firmly on a particular step and steady ourselves before we move on. We may be born with something inside us that makes this step more difficult than others; we may have needed extra help and did not get it. Or, we may have been pushed off the step by the insensitivity, impatience, or blindness of another person.

The beauty of the spiral is that we always get another chance. Encountering the step again at the same place in a higher rotation, we can learn to do it better the next time. We can become more sure-footed as we get older.

EXERCISE

Identifying Your Childhood Wound
Time: 30 minutes

OBJECTIVE

• To discover the nature of your childhood wounds.

You and your partner should complete this exercise separately.

When a child's developmental needs are not supported in a particular stage, the child develops a wound that manifests as a fear in intimate partnerships. The purpose of this exercise is to help you pinpoint in which stage or stages you were wounded as a child. When you know *what* the wound is, you can learn how to heal it.

Following you will find a list of the common fears people have when they were wounded in each particular stage of development. Read through the lists for all six stages and then return to the first one, Attachment Stage.

Read through the stages again, this time circling the one fear that you feel most often. You may have more than one fear, but choose the one that feels most powerful to you. Your choice will reveal how you may have been wounded in childhood and point to what needs to change in order for healing to begin.

1. Attachment Stage

    1a. I am sometimes afraid that my partner does not want me, and that he or she might reject me or leave me.

    1b. I am sometimes afraid of being abandoned, and that if I take time for myself, I will lose my relationship.

2. Exploration Stage

    2a. I am sometimes afraid of being smothered, absorbed, or humiliated by my partner.

    2b. I sometimes become afraid when my partner is unreliable—when he or she is sometimes there and sometimes not there for me.

3. Identity Stage

    3a. I am sometimes afraid of being shamed for being who I am and losing my partner's love.

    3b. I am sometimes afraid that if I give in to my partner, I will become invisible and lose my partner's love.

4. Competence Stage

    4a. I sometimes fear being seen as a failure, and that I have to prove my worth or risk losing my partner's approval and love.

    4b. I am sometimes afraid that if I am seen as aggressive, successful, competent, and powerful, I might lose my partner's love and acceptance.

5. Concern Stage

    5a. I am sometimes afraid that my partner does not see me as an equal and/or does not like me and does not want to be with me.

    5b. I am sometimes afraid that if I show my partner that I have needs and express them, my partner will exclude me.

6. Intimacy Stage

    6a. I am sometimes afraid that my partner wants to control me and I will not be free to express myself without being criticized.

    6b. I am sometimes afraid that I will not have my partner's approval because I am different from my partner and other people.

EXAMPLE:

When Sally and Jim responded to the questions above, Sally checked 6a. She was often frustrated by what she perceived as Jim's attempts to tell her what to do and what to think. His tendency to micromanage reminded Sally of her mother's insistence on doing the same.

What jumped out at Jim was 5b. It had already been pointed out to him by a concerned boss at work that he tended to go overboard in making sure everybody else was okay, while ignoring his own best interests. His boss said that Jim seemed to have a "driving need to be liked." Answering these questions helped him see that he was afraid Sally wouldn't love him if he was too vocal about expressing his own desires and needs.

EXERCISE
Learning More about How Your Childhood Wound Affects Your Relationship

Time: 30 minutes

OBJECTIVE

- To discover how your childhood wound has taken form in your life.

You and your partner may choose to do this step individually or together. This exercise will help you move from fear to growth and healing. Five different pieces of information are provided for each developmental stage. Once you have identified your primary fear, you will learn more about:

- Your relationship wound
- Your relationship defense
- Your character structure
- Your relationship growth challenge
- Your partner's profile

1. Attachment Stage
If you selected either 1a or 1b as your greatest fear: Your main wound was in the attachment stage of development, birth through eighteen months. In addition to food, what babies need most to survive are physical and emotional contact, and a reliable source of love and comfort. When babies do not get that consistent nurturing, they either become excessively clingy, or excessively detached.

If you selected 1a:

- *Your Relationship Wound:* Fear of rejection, and loss of self through contact with your partner.
- *Your Relationship Defense Is to Be an Avoider.* You tend to be detached and avoid social interaction. As an avoider, you probably fear too many feelings and chaos, and think contact will lead to rejection. This could be due to inadequate care during the age of attachment from birth through eighteen months. You might feel like you have no right to exist, and then withdraw and engage in obsessive thinking to attend to your needs. An avoidant or detached adult will believe: "I will be hurt if I initiate contact with you."
- *Your Character Structure Is to Be a Minimizer.* You tend to hold your emotions inside, inhibit general expressiveness toward others, and devalue expressiveness in yourself and others.
- *Your Relationship Growth Challenge:* Detached adults must learn to claim their right to *be,* and maintain connection, especially with their partners, by initiating emotional and physical contact, expressing feelings, and increasing body awareness and sensory contact with their environment.
- *Your Partner Tends to Be a Clinger.*

If you selected 1b:

- *Your Relationship Wound:* Fear of loss of self if you lose contact with your partner.
- *Your Relationship Defense Is to Be a Clinger.* You tend to cling to your partner and give him or her little breathing room. Your parents' inconsistent nurturing after your birth through eighteen months may have left you with a voracious appetite for connection and love. When conflicts arrive, you instinctually heighten demands to get your needs met, and you refuse to negotiate until you give in altogether. As an adult, a clinger will hold the following belief in relationship: "I am safe if I hold onto you."
- *Your Character Structure Is to Be a Maximizer.* You tend to exaggerate your emotions and general expressiveness toward others, and to overvalue expressiveness in yourself and others.
- *Your Relationship Growth Challenge:* Clingers must learn to focus on letting go, do things on their own, and negotiate while maintaining connection—especially within their partnerships.
- *Your Partner Tends to Be an Avoider.*

2. Exploration Stage

If you selected either 2a or 2b as your greatest fear: Your main wound was in the exploration stage of development, eighteen months through three years. A toddler mostly needs support and encouragement to explore his or her environment. When a toddler does not get the support and encouragement, he or she tends to be overly isolated or overly pursuing.

If you selected 2a:

- *Your Relationship Wound:* Fear of being smothered and losing self by merging with a partner.
- *Your Relationship Defense Is to Be an Isolator.* You tend to isolate yourself and protect your privacy. Your parents prevented you from exploring the world to the degree you desired. Love left you feeling smothered and humiliated, so you distanced yourself from loved ones. You wish to demand freedom, but are afraid of losing relationships. Thus, you resort to passive-aggressive tactics and suppress your rage. As an adult, an isolator will believe about relationships: "I can't say no and be loved, so I won't ask for anything."
- *Your Character Structure Is to Be a Minimizer.* You tend to withhold your emotions and general expressiveness toward others, and to devalue expressiveness in yourself and others.
- *Your Relationship Growth Challenge:* Isolators must focus on initiating closeness, sharing feelings, increasing time together, and integrating the negative and positive traits of their partners.
- *Your Partner Tends to Be a Pursuer.*

If you selected 2b:

- *Your Relationship Wound:* Fear of neglect and loss of your partner.
- *Your Relationship Defense Is to Be a Pursuer.* You tend to pursue your partner, invade his or her privacy, and act dependent. Wounded by caretakers who weren't always there when you returned from explorations, you equate independence with being abandoned. You may think that you can't count on anyone when you need support. You see your partner as distant and self-absorbed, and may frequently voice complaints, criticism, and fears when facing conflicts. You pursue, but then withdraw. A pursuer will have the belief: "If I act independently, you will abandon me."

- *Your Character Structure Is to Be a Maximizer.* You tend to exaggerate your emotions and general expressiveness toward others, and to overvalue expressiveness in yourself and others.
- *Your Growth Challenge:* Pursuers must learn to initiate separateness, develop outside interests, accept their partner, and integrate the positive and negative traits of their partner.
- *Your Partner Tends to Be an Isolator.*

3. Identity Stage

If you selected either 3a or 3b as your greatest fear: Your main wound was in the identity stage, ages three through four. When a young child is trying on new identities, the parent needs to mirror and validate whoever the child is being at the moment. When this supportive and safe atmosphere doesn't exist, the child becomes either a rigid controller or an invisible person with diffuse boundaries.

If you selected 3a:

- *Your Relationship Wound:* Fear of shame and loss of partner's love if you lose self-control or fail.
- *Your Relationship Defense Is to Be a Rigid Controller.* You attempt to control and manage your partner and others. Your childhood was likely full of discipline, rules, and shame, limiting your ability to form an identity that expressed all of you. In turn, you believe that you can't be yourself and be accepted. You feel compelled to take charge and lay down the law, though you don't enjoy it. You fear embarrassment due to your partner's nebulous desires, and can't bear the chaos, vulnerability, and passivity he or she brings to the relationship. As an adult, the rigid controller will believe about relationships: "I'll be safe if I stay in control."
- *Your Character Structure Is to Be a Minimizer.* You tend to withhold your emotions and general expressiveness toward others, and to devalue expressiveness in yourself and others.
- *Your Growth Challenge:* Rigid controllers must focus on relaxing their control, mirroring their partners' thoughts and feelings, and becoming more flexible and sensitive.
- *Your Partner Tends to Be a Compliant Diffuser.*

If you selected 3b:

- *Your Relationship Wound:* Fear of being ignored and becoming invisible, and therefore losing your partner's love.

- *Your Relationship Defense Is to Be a Compliant Diffuser.* You tend to be unclear and indirect. Alternately fearing invisibility and self-assertion, you adopt passive-aggressive methods to get the attention you secretly desire, and seek love by pleasing others. You resent your partner's control of the relationship, but are at a loss to make any suggestions. You exaggerate your emotions defiantly, and then become self-effacing and compliant. The invisible person with diffuse boundaries will have the following belief as an adult: "I'll be loved if I go along and please others."
- *Your Character Structure Is to Be a Maximizer.* You tend to exaggerate your emotions and general expressiveness toward others, and to overvalue expressiveness in yourself and others.
- *Your Growth Challenge:* People with diffuse boundaries must learn to assert themselves, set boundaries for themselves, and respect the boundaries of others—especially within their partnerships.
- *Your Partner Tends to Be a Rigid Controller.*

4. Competence Stage

If you selected either 4a or 4b as your greatest fear: Your main wound was in the competence stage of development, ages four through seven. At this stage, a child needs continued nurturing, plus warm and consistent praise for his or her efforts to master new skills. When this praise is not forthcoming, the child becomes either overly competitive or overly compromising.

If you selected 4a:

- *Your Relationship Wound:* Fear of being dominated by your partner and loss of love if you fail.
- *Your Relationship Defense Is to Be a Compulsive Competitor.* You tend to compete with everyone, including your partner, and you want to *win*. Your caretakers probably placed larger expectations on you than you were prepared to handle. They made you feel that you had to be perfect, and you became afraid that failure would result in loss of all love. You compete with your partner, but his or her weak and manipulative tactics frustrate you. You put your partner down ruthlessly and then feel guilty about it. The overly competitive child, as an adult, develops this belief about relationships: "I'll be loved if I am the best."
- *Your Character Structure Is to Be a Minimizer.* You tend to withhold your emotions and general expressiveness toward others, and to devalue expressiveness in yourself and others.
- *Your Relationship Growth Challenge:* People who are competitors must focus on accepting their competence and becoming cooperative, as well as mirroring and valuing their partners' efforts.

- *Your Partner Tends to Be a Manipulative Compromiser.*

If you selected 4b:

- *Your Relationship Wound:* Fear of being aggressive and powerful because engaging in rivalry will lead to the loss of your partner's approval.
- *Your Relationship Defense Is to Be a Manipulative Compromiser.* You tend to devalue yourself, withhold your opinions, and compromise. You may think your partner is never satisfied and doesn't respect your contributions to the relationship. It's hard to get the respect you desire, because you naturally adopt a compromising role, thinking goodness and cooperation will lead to love. Your partner's more aggressive nature makes you feel helpless and resentful, so you resort to manipulation to get your needs met. The overly compromising child has this belief as an adult: "I'll be loved if I am good and cooperative."
- *Your Character Structure Is to Be a Maximizer.* You tend to exaggerate your emotions and general expressiveness toward others, and to overvalue expressiveness in yourself and others.
- *Your Relationship Growth Challenge:* Compromisers must learn to be direct, express power, develop competence, and praise their partner's successes.
- *Your Partner Tends to Be a Compulsive Competitor.*

5. Concern Stage

If you selected either 5a or 5b as your greatest fear: Your main wound occurred in the concern stage, ages seven through twelve. The older child needs wisdom and guidance from parents, but also the space and time to integrate connection with his or her peers. If this does not happen, the child can become either an excessive loner or an excessive caretaker.

If you selected 5a:

- *Your Relationship Wound:* You fear being rejected by your partner and ostracized by your peers.
- *Your Relationship Defense Is to Be a Loner.* You tend to withdraw and, when hurt, to refuse nurturing; in the same way, you tend to exclude your partner. You may believe that you're truly unlovable and fear the agony that closeness will arouse. Your partner, however, seeks you out and tries to intrude on your lonely world. You might avoid him or her and reject his or her overtures, but you must confront the pain of self-exile in order to escape depression and loneliness. As an adult, the loner believes about relationships: "I'll be hurt if I try to be too close."

- *Your Character Structure Is to Be a Minimizer.* You tend to withhold your emotions and general expressiveness toward others, and to devalue expressiveness in yourself and others.
- *Your Relationship Growth Challenge:* Loners must learn to become inclusive, develop same-sex friends, and enjoy socializing by sharing feelings and thoughts with others, especially their partners.
- *Your Partner Tends to Be a Sacrificial Caretaker.*

If you selected 5b:

- *Your Relationship Wound:* You fear rejection or exclusion if you express your needs.
- *Your Relationship Defense Is to Be a Sacrificial Caretaker.* You tend to serve others and meet their needs, while denying and ignoring your own. As a child, you found that loved ones who rejected your gestures of concern caused you to feel hurt. You still find yourself with a partner who excludes you from the essential part of his or her life and fails to reciprocate your love. This leads to resentment and depression as you struggle to meet his or her needs. The sacrificial caretaker believes: "I'll be loved if I meet your needs."
- *Your Character Structure Is to Be a Maximizer.* You tend to exaggerate your emotions and general expressiveness toward others, and to overvalue the expressiveness in yourself and others.
- *Your Relationship Growth Challenge:* Sacrificial Caretakers must learn to express their needs to their partner and others, practice self-care, respect their partner's privacy, and take time to be alone.
- *Your Partner Tends to Be a Loner.*

6. Intimacy Stage

If you selected either 6a or 6b as your greatest fear: Your main wound occurred in the intimacy stage, ages twelve through eighteen. The teenager needs to be surrounded by a family where people regularly share feelings and thoughts, and communication is natural. When this does not happen, the teenager can become either a rebel or a conformist.

If you selected 6a:

- *Your Relationship Wound:* Fear of losing personal freedom and being controlled by your partner and others.
- *Your Relationship Defense Is to Be a Rebel.* You tend to challenge instructions, rebel against authority, and act out your feelings. Fearing oppression and conformity all

around, you recall parents who didn't let you break the rules. You may think no one trusts you and that growing up equals selling out. Your partner is a generally self-righteous follower who tires of your flamboyant outbursts. You want everyone to be on your side, but you can't trust anyone who's nice to you. Rebels, as adults, share this belief about relationships: "I'll be controlled if I give up dissent."

- *Your Character Structure Is to Be a Minimizer.* You tend to withhold your emotions and general expressiveness toward others, and to devalue expressiveness in yourself and in others.
- *Your Relationship Growth Challenge:* Rebels need to maintain their identities, be responsible to others, and learn to trust others, especially their partner.
- *Your Partner Tends to Be a Conformist.*

If you selected 6b:

- *Your Relationship Wound:* Fear that if you are different and express your uniqueness, you will lose your partner's approval and the approval of others.
- *Your Relationship Defense Is to Be a Conformist.* You try to be like others by always being agreeable and avoiding risks. Wounded in this stage of intimacy, you fear disapproval and being different. You believe you have to be good and hold things together in order to survive. The childish rebelliousness of your partner threatens the stability and normalcy you crave, but his or her freedom and zealousness attract you. Nevertheless, you rely on condescending and reactionary behavior to place boundaries around the relationship. Conformists, as adults, believe this about relationships: "I have to hold things together."
- *Your Character Structure Is to Be a Maximizer.* You tend to exaggerate your emotions and general expressiveness toward others, and to overvalue expressiveness in yourself and others.
- *Your Relationship Growth Challenge:* Conformists need to experiment with being different from others, take more risks, and develop their identities, especially within their partnership.
- *Your Partner Tends to Be a Rebel.*

EXAMPLE:

When Sally read her profile in 6a, she made these discoveries: She was afraid of being controlled. She was supersensitive to whatever Jim did that felt like he might want to control her. When she was unhappy, she tended to withdraw and withhold. She realized that her challenge was to learn to trust Jim.

When Jim read his profile in 5b, this is what he discovered: He was afraid Sally would reject him if he seemed weak. He tended to be the caretaker in his relationship with

Sally. He overcompensated for Sally's reticence by being overly expressive. He needed to work on taking care of himself by admitting to himself what he wanted and needed, and by telling Sally more of what was in his heart.

EXERCISE

What to Do with Information About Your Childhood Wound

Time: 30 minutes

OBJECTIVE

- To turn unconscious reactions to your childhood wound in your relationship into conscious actions.

STEP 1.

Using the Imago Dialogue, share your discoveries from the previous exercises with your partner. Choose a time and place that works for both of you. Decide who will be the Sender and who will be the Receiver. Then, follow this process:

- The Sender tells the Receiver which fear he or she identified in Exercise 1 as being most significant. For example, Sally would refer to page 109, which discusses 6a, the fear she chose as most significant for herself. The Sender can add any additional comments that would help clarify his or her thoughts, feelings, and experiences around the fear.
- The Receiver mirrors what the Sender has just said, and asks, *"Did I get that right?"*
- If the Receiver mirrored accurately, the Sender continues by summarizing what he or she has learned in Exercise 2 about the childhood wound that corresponds to the fear, and the information it suggests about their relationship.
- The Receiver mirrors and checks to see if the mirror is accurate.
- If the Receiver mirrored accurately, he or she asks if there is more the Sender wants to say.
- If not, then the Receiver proceeds to the steps of validating and empathizing.
- Then switch places, and it is the Sender's turn to receive and the Receiver's turn to send, following the same process as before.

STEP 2.

Your dialogue will include sharing information on your Relationship Growth Challenge, which is included in Exercise 2. Your relationship growth challenge can be transformed into a goal for your behavior in your relationship. It essentially tells you what new behavior you will want to develop in order to build a more satisfying relationship.

Write your relationship growth challenge in the form of a goal and add at least three specific actions you will take to achieve this goal. A goal is written as an "I" statement that articulates something positive you intend to achieve for the good of your relationship. Here are some examples of goal statements: "I will be a more cooperative and less competitive partner." "I will become a good listener." "I will validate my partner more." "I will be accepting, rather than judgmental." "I will become a more actively involved partner."

Under your goal statement, also write down when or how often you intend to perform the actions you've identified. Use the following form to turn your relationship growth challenge into a concrete plan.

CONCRETE PLAN FOR YOUR RELATIONSHIP GROWTH CHALLENGE

My Relationship Growth Challenge Goal is: _____

_____

_____

_____

Three specific actions I will take to achieve this goal are:

1. I will _____

_____

_____

_____

Indicate time by when you will do this, or how often: _____

_____

_____

_____

2. I will _____

_____

_____

_____

Indicate time by when you will do this, or how often: _____

_____

_____

_____

3. I will _____

_____

_____

_____

Indicate time by when you will do this, or how often: _____

_____

_____

_____

Keep what you have written in a place where you'll be reminded of it constantly. Refer to it often and revise the actions you need to take to keep moving toward your goal. When you have successfully completed one of your actions, pause and congratulate yourself. Take time to celebrate your accomplishments.

EXAMPLE:

Sally's relationship growth challenge was, "I want to learn to trust Jim." She rewrote it as a goal this way: "I will trust Jim." Her three actions and their time frames were: (1) I will write down at least one instance every day when Jim keeps his word. I will do this for one month. (2) I will move beyond my comfort zone and tell Jim something that is hard for me to say, and that I would have hidden from him in the past. I will expose myself like this at least once a week for the next 8 weeks. (3) I will tell Jim when I feel mistrustful and let him reassure me. I will do this at least once a week for the next 8 weeks.

Sally wrote this down on a piece of paper and put it in the front of her journal. Since she was an avid journaler, she was often reminded of the changes she wanted to make in her behavior.

*Jim's relationship growth challenge was, "I need to work on taking care of myself by admitting to myself what I want and need, and by telling Sally more of what is in my heart." He rewrote it as a goal this way: "I want to be more real about who I am." His three actions and their time frames were: (1) I will tell Sally that I want to make some changes in my daily routine, such as going to sleep earlier, skipping wine with dinner on work nights, and getting up half an hour earlier in the morning to do my weight-lifting routine. I will ask for a dialogue within the next five days about these changes. I will then ask for a dialogue about these changes once a week for the next two months. (2) I will be more honest about how I want to spend my recreational "down" time. The next time she asks what I want to do on the weekend, I will tell her my real preferences instead of saying what I think **she'd** like to do. If she doesn't bring this subject up in the next week, I will. I will continue to practice this every week for the next two months. (3) I will express at least one purely selfish desire every week. I will do this once a week for the next month.*

BETWEEN-SESSION ASSIGNMENTS

The Concrete Plan for Your Relationship Growth Challenge that you formulated above is one of your most important tools for changing your behavior in positive ways.

- At least once every week, review your progress toward achieving your goal by checking whether you have accomplished one or all three of your specific steps.
- Share your progress with your partner, and invite him or her to share theirs.
- Periodically update the steps you have written down to achieve your goal. When you achieve one, cross it out. If it makes sense to do so, add others that are relevant. Remember, growth is an ongoing, lifetime process, and not just a specific accomplishment.
- Return to the activities of the first session. At least once this week, share with your partner what you have added to your Daily Gift Record. See Session 1, page 20, for instructions. In addition, at least once this week, share with your partner what you have written down on your partner's Dream Gift List. See page 22 for instructions.

Identifying Your Defenses

REVIEW IN *RECEIVING LOVE*

Chapter 4, "The Present Is a Window into the Past," pages 73–74, and "The Personal Consequences of the Split Self," pages 79–82

Chapter 5, "Connecting the Dots," pages 104–106, and "Rejecting Love in Committed Relationships," pages 106–119

TIME FRAME

Approximately 20 minutes

SPECIAL CONSIDERATIONS

In the last session, you had a chance to understand more clearly how you were wounded as a child. Now, you will have the opportunity to see how your wounds caused you to develop certain defenses. The problem with defenses is that they often have a destructive effect in intimate relationships. Knowing what your defenses are, and making conscious decisions about when and how to change them, is a healing step.

WHAT YOU NEED TO KNOW

All of us try to stay safe in the face of physical danger through a variety of defensive reactions, including flight, fighting, playing dead, and surrendering. We share these defenses with a variety of other animals and revert to them when we feel threatened. In addition to these biological reactions to physical threats, human beings are capable of developing other defenses to protect themselves from *psychological* dangers. Psychological dangers are more prevalent for us than physical ones, appearing whenever we perceive assaults to our concept of ourselves as decent, competent people.

It is very threatening for us to acknowledge that we are still "works in progress." We are not fully evolved. We still have things to work on. We make mistakes. We have areas where we are still undeveloped. And yet making peace with our failings and fears is so painful, we don't want to do it. Instead, we try to maintain a façade of control and invulnerability by using any combination of the six psychological defenses: denial of the negative, disowning the positive, deflecting the positive, projecting traits and motives onto others, defending against seeing the otherness of others, and protecting from symbiosis. Two definitions you may need to more completely understand these six defenses are: (1) projection, the tendency to assign to another person feelings, thoughts, or attitudes that are actually present in yourself, and (2) symbiosis, absorbing the thoughts or feelings of another person in such a way that it is difficult to function as an independent person, or allow the other person to be independent.

The reality is that we were all wounded in childhood. All of us have been eroded by difficult experiences. Some of us have been fortunate enough to begin to repair the damage and restore our wholeness. Some of us are just learning how to do this. But, in either case, we are probably still caught in a web of defensiveness. We try to compensate for our fragile sense of self by doing whatever we can to appear blameless and without fault. We desperately want to appear acceptable to others so we can feel better about ourselves.

Reparation and renewal cannot begin without self-knowledge. We have to know what we are trying to protect ourselves from and what defenses we are using as weapons before we can relax our guard. The following exercise will assist you in identifying some of the defenses you may resort to when you feel psychologically threatened.

EXERCISE

How Do You Try to Defend Yourself?

Time: 20 minutes

OBJECTIVE

• To become aware of the defenses you use to try to protect yourself in your relationships.

You and your partner should complete this exercise separately, and then share your findings with each other in Step 7.

STEP 1.

There are many ways to try to protect your fragile sense of self. Below is a list of six defenses that people commonly employ when they are confronted with a perceived assault to their self-esteem. Under each defense are examples of the kinds of statements people make when they are operating within that particular defense.

Read through the list of all six defenses, and think about whether the examples correspond to things you often say and think. Put a check mark by each statement you have used within recent memory. Write down any additional statements that you can recall making that are not on this list.

1. Denial of the negative.

_____I didn't do it.

_____

_____

_____I am never that way.

_____

_____

_____It's not my fault.

_____

_____

Additional Statements:

_____

_____

_____

2. Disowning the positive.

_____I can't do that.

_____

_____

_____I don't have the ability.

_____

_____

_____I wish I were like that.

_____

_____

Additional Statements:

_____

_____

_____

3. Deflecting the positive.

_____I am not that good.

_____

_____

_____I don't deserve it.

_____

_____

_____I can't have it.

_____

_____

Additional Statements:

_____

_____

_____

4. Projecting traits and motives onto others.

_____I'm not angry, you are.

_____

_____

_____You are not a caring person.

_____

_____

_____You don't want to listen to me.

_____

_____

Additional Statements:

_____

_____

5. Defending against seeing the otherness of others.

_____You don't think that.

_____

_____

_____You don't want that.

_____

_____

_____You don't feel that.

_____

_____

Additional Statements:

_____

_____

_____

6. Protecting from symbiosis.

_____I don't see it that way.

_____

_____

_____I don't like that.

_____

_____

_____I won't agree with you.

_____

_____

Additional Statements:

_____

_____

_____

STEP 2.

Go back to the statements you've checked or added. In the blank lines provided under each one, write down a brief description of the occasion you remember saying or thinking that particular phrase.

EXAMPLE:

*Although Linda could relate to several of the defensive statements above, two of them struck her as particularly descriptive of her reaction to a perceived threat. Under #1, denial of the negative, Linda remembered when Lonnie told their neighbor that she was afraid to say No when people asked her to do something. Linda remembered thinking, "I am never that way." And under #4, projecting traits and motives onto others, Linda remembered slamming the door one night last week when she was mad at Lonnie for being rude to her mother on the phone. She was quite angry, when she accused **him** of being angry.*

Lonnie chose two others as sounding most like him. Under #1, denial of the negative, he had to admit that he was quick to point the finger at other people when he thought he was going to be in trouble. In fact, he would often say, "It's not my fault." Under #5, defending against seeing the otherness of others, Lonnie admitted that he thought he had Linda all figured out. He thought he knew her better than she did herself, and would often tell her, "You don't think that."

STEP 3.

Notice that all the examples you noted in Step 1 are negative statements about the self or a behavior. They are statements of denial. An effective way to counter your defenses and reclaim all parts of yourself is to accept the totality of who you are. You can do that by changing the negative language of your defenses into positive language. Here again are the six defenses from Step 1, but this time they've been changed into their positive opposites.

1. Accepting the negative.

> I did do it.
>
> I sometimes am that way.
>
> I am responsible.

2. Owning the positive.

> I can do that.
>
> I do have the ability.
>
> I am like that.

3. Accepting the positive.

> I am that good.
>
> I deserve it.
>
> I can have it.

4. Owning traits and motives assigned to others.

> I am the one who is angry.
>
> Sometimes I really am an uncaring person.
>
> I see I am the one who doesn't want to listen to you.

5. Seeing the otherness of others.

> I can see that you think that.
>
> I accept that you don't want that.
>
> I understand that you feel that way.

6. Joining with others.

> I can see it that way.
>
> I will learn to like that, too.
>
> I can agree with you.

STEP 4.

Now go back and reimagine the occasions when you remembered using your defenses (you wrote them down on the blank lines of Step 1, during Step 2) and think about what would have been different if you had used a positive statement of acceptance, instead of the negative defense.

> *EXAMPLE:*
>
> *For Linda, "I am never that way" became "well, okay, it's true that I do sometimes have trouble saying No, but I'm working on it." She realized that if she doesn't admit that it's a problem, she can't change it. "I'm not angry, you are" became "It would have felt more honest if I had told you that I was angry at you last Friday for being abrupt with my mother on the phone. If I'd told you that, maybe I would have gotten over it sooner, because you wouldn't have gotten mad at me for denying that I was angry."*

Lonnie decided he wanted to start taking more responsibility for his actions. Whenever he was tempted to blurt out, "It's not my fault," he paused, and remembered his promise to be more discerning and more honest about his actions and decisions. Lonnie came to understand that assuming he knew how his wife thought was, at the very least, disrespectful. "You don't think that" became "Maybe I can guess what you're thinking, but I need to ask you to make sure, and to get a more accurate picture of who you are."

STEP 5.

We are unconscious of so much of our hurtful behavior. For this reason, it's now time for you and your partner to fill out this exercise *for each other*. Go back to Step 1. Check the defenses you think *your partner* has employed in the recent past, and your partner can check the defenses he or she thinks *you* have used. Proceed to Step 2, giving your partner examples of when he or she used those defenses. Your partner will do the same for you. Remember, those closest to you can often see your defensive reactions better than you can.

EXAMPLE:

*Under #5, defending against seeing the otherness of others, Linda thought Lonnie was quick to tell her, "You don't feel that way." This was interesting, because it is in the same family of defenses that Lonnie identified for himself. Linda remembered him telling her in the recent past, when they had to turn down a dinner invitation, "You must feel bad about that," when actually she didn't. She thought maybe **he** felt bad about it. Under #6, protecting from symbiosis, Linda was often frustrated when it seemed to her that Lonnie was refusing to agree with something, out of sheer orneriness.*

Lonnie checked #2, disowning the positive, for Linda. It bothered him when she said, "I wish I were like that." The last time it happened, she was bemoaning the fact that she didn't volunteer in the kids' school as often as she thought she should. Lonnie also checked #3, deflecting the positive, for Linda. In his view, she didn't know how to accept a compliment. The tone she adopted was, "I'm not that good."

Once you've completed Step 2, review Step 3, and proceed to Step 4 to what would have been different if your partner had a positive statement of acceptance instead of the negative defense.

STEP 6.

This step is about setting your intention to drop your defenses and accept yourselves as you really are. You can use the following form to make your behavior goals (as expressed by you in Step 4, and in later steps by your partner) concrete. Filling out the form will also deepen your understanding of the discoveries you've made about your defenses in this session, by having you put them in your own words. You and your partner should both fill out one form each and share with each other in Step 7.

The combination of the defenses you are aware of using and examples from your partner will give you a fairly complete picture of the ways you try to protect yourself from information about your lack of wholeness. Confronting this and turning your current negative statements to positive ones will be healing.

BEHAVIOR GOALS FOR YOUR DEFENSES

From now on, when I'm feeling (enter an example of a negative feeling from Step 2),

_____

_____

_____

_____

I will pause and ask myself (whether my feeling is really a defense).

_____

_____

_____

I will try to be honest and accepting of myself and acknowledge when (refer back to the list of positive statements in Step 3)

_____

_____

_____

_____

Instead of what I have done in the past, which is to be defensive and (refer back to the list of the six defenses in Step 1), I will (behavior goal)

_____

_____

_____

_____

EXAMPLE:

This is how Linda filled out the form with regard to her "I'm not angry, you are" defense:

- From now on when I'm feeling *that you're mad at me,* I will pause and ask myself if I am the one who is angry.
- I will try to be honest and accepting of myself and acknowledge when *I am the one who is angry, and not you.*
- Instead of what I have done in the past, which is to be defensive *and blame my anger on you,* I will *cop to my own angry feeling.*

This is how Lonnie filled out the form with regard to his "You don't think that" defense:

- From now on when I'm feeling that *you don't know what you are thinking,* I will pause and ask myself *whether I am assuming things about you I don't know.*
- I will try to be honest and accepting of myself and acknowledge when *I am not being respectful that you are an individual separate from me.*
- Instead of what I have done in the past, which is to be defensive and assume I know everything about you, *I will ask you what you are feeling.*

STEP 7.

In the new partnership you and your partner are forming, you will be able to help each other stay the course toward less defensiveness and more self-acceptance. You can learn to coach each other away from old behaviors and toward new, healthier ones.

Using the Imago Dialogue, share your discoveries from the previous exercises with your partner. Choose a time and place that works for both of you. Decide who will be the Sender and who will be the Receiver. Then, follow this process:

- The Sender tells the Receiver which fear he or she identified in Exercise 1 as being most significant. For example, if Linda were the Sender and she wanted to tell Lonnie how she intends to deal with her defense of accusing him of being angry when she is the one who is angry, she would refer to her Behavior Goals. She would tell him why she wants to transform this defense to recognition of her own anger, using examples, and adding any additional comments that would help clarify her message.
- The Receiver mirrors what the Sender has just said, and asks, "Did I get that right?"
- If the Receiver mirrored accurately, the Sender continues by summarizing what he or she has learned in Exercise 2 about the childhood wound that corresponds to the fear, and the information it suggests about their relationship.
- The Receiver mirrors and checks to see if the mirror is accurate.
- If the Receiver mirrored accurately, he or she asks if there is more the Sender wants to say.
- If not, then the Receiver proceeds to the steps of validating and empathizing.
- Then switch places, and it is the Sender's turn to receive and the Receiver's turn to send, following the same process as before.

BETWEEN-SESSION ASSIGNMENTS

- On at least two occasions each week, tell your partner about times when you were tempted to react defensively, and instead, were able to respond with more self-acceptance and more honesty. Describe how you were able to reimagine yourself in your new role as a person who knows and accepts who he or she is.
- Periodically review your responses on the form in Step 6, pages 125–126, so you can remind yourself of what conscious responses you want to replace your unconscious defensive reactions.
- In Session 3, you had the opportunity to understand whether you tend to approach the world as a separate or connected knower. If you concluded you were more of a separate knower, return to page 41 and follow the instructions for expanding your connected knowing abilities. If you concluded you were a connected knower, return to page 44 and follow the instructions for expanding your separate knowing abilities.

Discovering Your Hidden Potential

REVIEW IN *RECEIVING LOVE*

Chapter 3, "Where Do You Stand?" pages 70–71

Chapter 4, "Splitting Leads to Self-Rejection," pages 74–77

TIME FRAME

Approximately 30 minutes for each exercise for a total of 1 hour

SPECIAL CONSIDERATIONS

This session gives you the chance to become aware of the messages you have received from parents, caretakers, and partners about how you should function as a human being. You will focus on five areas of functioning—thinking, feeling, sensing, moving, and core being. This session will give you the opportunity to understand how much of each area of functioning was lost to you because of negative messages you received from others. The session moves from negative messages you received in childhood, to negative messages you and your partner have gotten from each other, and, finally, to converting negative messages into positive ones.

WHAT YOU NEED TO KNOW

In our newborn state, we have the capability of using our bodies and minds to interact with our environment. We can take in and send out information with our minds, feel and express our emotions, interact with our environment through our five senses, and move our muscles in all sorts of ways. We are born with full potential within the "four functions of the self," which are: thinking, feeling, sensing, and moving. These functions are all connected and work together seamlessly. And, through them, we are connected to everything—other people, our environment, the universe, and that from which it all originated and is sustained.

For most of us, however, this wholeness and connectedness is short-lived. To develop and sustain our connection with ourselves and our environment, we need attuned and supportive caretakers and peers. We are relationally dependent. Unfortunately, as a species, we have not yet evolved to the point where we can rear our children without rupturing their connection to themselves and to everything else in their environment. Caretakers, unconsciously and with the best of intentions, assist or impede the development of their children through the messages they give them.

For instance, our caretakers may have told us that it's okay to use our brains to think, or they may have ignored, deflected, or criticized our thinking. They may have honored our feelings and thus confirmed their validity, or they may have told us not to feel at all, or to feel only *certain* feelings. Some caretakers may have encouraged their children to use their senses and modeled how to look at flowers and smell their aromas, listen to music, appreciate the flavor of food, and enjoy the warmth of touch. Others may have ignored the senses and deflected or devalued sensory curiosity. Some caretakers may have encouraged their children to move their muscles, to dance, or be athletic, while others conveyed the message to be still and not to run.

The functions that are impeded or ignored by our caretakers fail to develop. They are lost to our awareness, but they do not disappear as potential. Their loss in childhood results in a split in the self that we are calling the "lost self." The lost self is never truly gone. It continues on in the unconscious, where it is influential in the selection of a partner and in the quality of the relationship that is formed with that partner.

Unlike the disowned self and the denied self, which are visible either to ourselves or to others, the lost self is not only out of our awareness, it is also out of the awareness of others (see Session 12 for more information about the disowned and denied selves). Thus, we can neither receive input nor express these missing functions in our relationships because those channels of relating are not open for giving and receiving. Their loss also interferes with relational knowing, and depending upon which functions are missing, we become either predominantly separate or connected knowers.

Whether the disowned, denied, and lost parts of ourselves are visible or invisible to ourselves and others, they play a major part in our drama of nonreceiving. People can't receive love because they can't accept positive input for traits, talents, and qualities they've disowned, denied, or lost, and they can't receive gifts their parents didn't approve of their having, for whatever reason. In other words, self-rejection and self-hatred block their ability to take in what would be healing.

It's logical to think that the solution would be to start loving yourself. Self-love is worth several billion dollars a year to the economy. Books, videos, audiotapes, and counselors are everywhere encouraging us to be good to ourselves. Write down personal affirmations, go to a spa, take time out, or take a hot bath. This is wonderful advice. And it feels good, at least temporarily. The problem is that conscious self-love, self-care, and self-soothing does not help people start loving the parts of them they've disowned, denied, or lost. They don't bring the rejected parts of the self back to the fold of consciousness. They don't erase the internalized disapproval of the parent that is activated when they try to get something for themselves that feels forbidden.

You cannot heal your disconnection by loving other people or by loving God. You may compensate for your self-hatred by loving others, but you do not heal the breach within yourself. The true corrective lies along a different path. You must start loving *in your partner* those traits, habits, attitudes, and behaviors that give you the most trouble, in fact the very things he or she does that drive you crazy. It could be anything: quickness to anger, tendency toward inertia, constant judgment, drive toward perfection, emphasis on appearances, recourse to grandiosity, or the habit of self-deprecation. Day to day, it could be the need to pick up the check always (or never), the need to brag about the children, the need to hide behind humor, or the need to be busy always (or never).

What do your partner's faults have to do with your lost self? The answer lies in the mechanism of projection. What you never developed, you tend to project onto others, with the most on-target projections aimed at your partner. In order to continue to relate to the parts of yourself that are missing, you project them onto your partner and relate to them in that form. You can experience the disapproval and dislike you have for yourself by disapproving and disliking those same things in your mate. This sounds far-fetched only because most projections are created in the unconscious. You don't know you're doing it.

However, it's not that you are making all these traits up completely and pasting them on your partner at random. You're not hallucinating when you think your partner is doing "that thing" again. There is almost always something in your partner that attracts your projections; this provides there is something for your projections to stick to. After all, you chose your partner based on your imago, or internalized image of a parent or primary caregiver, in the first place. And that means that during the power struggle, your partner really does demonstrate characteristics similar to the ones that created your lost self when you were young. Those traits really exist to some extent in your partner, and when you encounter them, they are supercharged.

PART I: Recovering Your Lost Self

In most intimate relationships, the functions you rejected in yourself are the opposite of those rejected by your partner in him or herself as a result of his or her caretakers' messages. This means that what is missing in you is developed in your partner. Because the functions that are "on-line" in your partner are "off-line" in you, you tend to reject those functions in your partner because your caretakers forbade them in you. In other words, you take the same negative attitude toward those functions in your partner that your caretakers took toward them in you. You will ask your partner, through criticism and devaluation, to sacrifice those same parts that you surrendered in order to survive in your family. And if you have children, you may find yourself asking your children to inhibit or repress aspects of themselves similar to the ones you were asked to inhibit or repress.

Initially, you were probably attracted to that part of your partner that you repressed in yourself. As time went on, though, it was precisely the characteristics that first attracted you that now frustrate and repel you. For example, if your experience with your caretakers resulted in you inhibiting your thinking, you will be attracted to a person whose thinking function is fully expressive and alive. This is true even though your partner's cognitive predisposition is something that eventually grates on your nerves. Without realizing you're doing it, you will ask your partner to limit, inhibit, or repress his or her thinking. You will do this unconsciously, even though you may want your partner to be free in the areas in which you were inhibited.

You cannot give your partner the permission you were denied, because your unconscious will prevent it. Since the function was denied to you, you will unconsciously deny it to your partner. The way out of this bind is to become conscious of aspects of self lost to you and repossess them.

EXERCISE

Identifying Your Lost Self

Time: 30 minutes

OBJECTIVES

- To determine which parts of your potential are hidden from you.

- To recapture the full functioning of your mind and body.

STEP 1.

In the columns below, record the positive and negative messages you received from your caretakers about each aspect of yourself listed in each column. Study the examples below before you start. They will guide you in doing the exercise.

EXAMPLES:

THINKING: Statements from caretakers:
Quit trying to make things so complicated.
Do you think you're smarter than we are?
We don't go in for that highbrow kind of stuff.
Message: Don't think.
I love how you made all these connections that I didn't see.
I like talking to you, because it helps me see a different perspective.
Wow! That is really good thinking.
Message: It's okay to think, to use your mind.

FEELING: Statements from caretakers:
Why don't you just calm down.
Not now. I don't want to hear it.
Don't get so hysterical.
Message: Don't feel (or feel certain feelings).
I want to know how you're feeling.
Are you feeling sad (worried, angry, etc.)?
I'm feeling sad about it. How about you?
Message: It's okay to feel your feelings.

SENSES: Statements from caretakers:
What are you, an arty type?
Don't waste time on that kind of stuff. We have work to do.
Caring about that is self-indulgent.
Message: Don't experience your senses.
You have such a good eye!
I knew you would appreciate this beautiful view.
I want to encourage your music (or your art, or your cooking).
Message: It's okay to use all your senses.

ACTION: Statements from caretakers:
Can't you just be quiet for once?
Just sit still and be a good little boy.
You're driving me crazy with all your fidgeting.
Message: Don't move your muscles.
Would you like to take a dancing class (or go out for sports)?
Wow! You climbed up those rocks really fast.
I'll bet you could hike around that lake in no time.
Message: It's okay to move your body.

CORE SELF: (Your real self): Statements from caretakers:
                  Don't be.
                  Don't.
                  Don't be you.
                  Don't want things.
                  Message: Don't exist.
                  It's okay to be.
                  It's okay to be you.
                  It's okay to be all of who you are.
                  Message: It's okay to exist.

MESSAGES I GOT FROM MY CARETAKERS
ABOUT ASPECTS OF MY SELF

Thinking	Feeling	Sensing	Moving	Core Self

Use the chart above to record the messages you received from your caretakers. Identify the positive messages with a + sign and the negative messages with a – sign. Count the total number of positive messages you received about each function and the total number of negative messages you received about each one. See the example below.

EXAMPLE:

Andy didn't think much about his childhood until he reached a personal crisis when he was in his forties. He experienced the loss of his business and his marriage, which caused him to examine his own attitudes about what it meant to be successful. He realized that he had adopted his father's hardworking ethic of masculinity and had denied the part of himself that was playful and nurturing.

Thinking	Feeling	Sensing	Moving	Core Self
– You're not so smart so you'll have to work harder – Don't depend on intuition – There is only one right way + Be logical	– Feelings are annoyances – Don't be vulnerable – Don't indulge yourself in your emotions – Don't let anybody know how you really feel	– Sex is a reward for working hard and making a lot of money – People in the arts are there because they can't do anything else	+ Be a good athlete + Be physically strong + Don't quit	– It's not safe to reveal who you really are – We don't care who you really are, be like your father

STEP 2.

On the diagram, record the number of negative and positive messages you received from your caretakers for each function. Study your negative messages for each function and black out your estimate of the percentage of that function you feel was repressed in your childhood.

The sections of the circle that you black out as repressed functions constitute your "lost self." These functions were rejected by your caretakers and thus by you. The remaining white space reflects the percent of that function that was not repressed.

MY LOST SELF FUNCTIONS

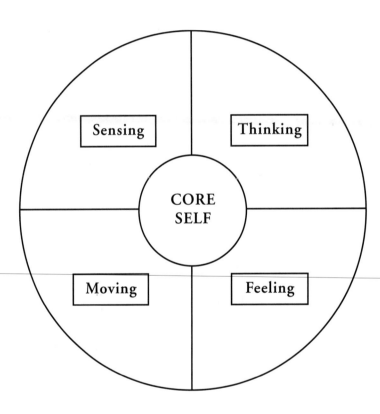

ANDY'S LOST SELF FUNCTIONS

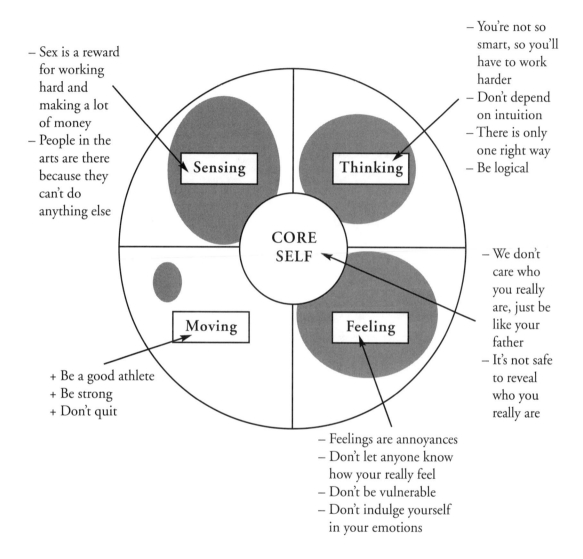

– Sex is a reward
  for working
  hard and
  making a lot
  of money
– People in the
  arts are there
  because they
  can't do
  anything else

– You're not so
  smart, so you'll
  have to work
  harder
– Don't depend
  on intuition
– There is only
  one right way
– Be logical

Sensing

Thinking

CORE SELF

– We don't
  care who
  you really
  are, just be
  like your
  father
– It's not safe
  to reveal
  who you
  really are

Moving

Feeling

+ Be a good athlete
+ Be strong
+ Don't quit

– Feelings are annoyances
– Don't let anyone know
  how your really feel
– Don't be vulnerable
– Don't indulge yourself
  in your emotions

You can see that Andy grew up with a large part of himself lost to his consciousness. His individuality was discouraged, and his conformity to his family's ideas about what it meant to be a successful man caused him to repress his experimental, expressive, intuitive side.

STEP 3.

Use the Imago Dialogue to share your discoveries about your lost self with your partner. Choose a time and place that works for both of you. Decide who will be the Sender and who will be the Receiver. Then, follow this process:

- The Sender tells the Receiver about the childhood messages that had an impact on which part of his or her functioning was lost. For example, if Andy were the Sender, he would tell his partner why so much of his feeling function was lost to him, and contrast that with how much of his moving function remained. He would give examples and add any additional comments that would help clarify his message.
- The Receiver mirrors what the Sender has just said, and asks, "Did I get that right?"
- If the Receiver mirrored accurately, the Sender continues by summarizing what he or she has learned in Exercise 2 about the childhood wound that corresponds to the fear, and the information it suggests about their relationship.
- The Receiver mirrors and checks to see if the mirror is accurate.
- If the Receiver mirrored accurately, he or she asks if there is more the Sender wants to say.
- If not, then the Receiver proceeds to the steps of validating and empathizing.
- Then switch places, and it is the Sender's turn to receive and the Receiver's turn to send, following the same process as before.

PART II: Recovering Your Lost Self in Relationship

Go through the same process you completed in Part I, except instead of recording which messages you received from your caretakers, *record the messages you send to your partner.*

EXERCISE

What Messages Do I Send to My Partner?

Time: 30 minutes

OBJECTIVE

- To learn how to interact with the hidden aspects of yourself and your partner as you build an intimate relationship together.

STEP 1.

Think about the statements you make to your partner about his or her freedom to think, to feel feelings, to experience the five senses, to move, and to be his or her core self. Fill out the chart below by recording both the positive and negative messages you've given to your partner.

Thinking	Feeling	Sensing	Moving	Core Self

EXAMPLE:

After Andy had thought about the messages he had received from his parents about his functioning, it was easier for him to see which messages he had passed on to his wife, Erica. Before this session, he hadn't been aware that he was sending her any messages at all. Although he realized that he had sent positive messages over the years, it was the negative messages that captured his attention. This is how he filled out the chart for the negative messages he thought he had sent Erica.

Thinking	Feeling	Sensing	Moving	Core Self
– *You're not as smart as I am.*	– *You are too emotional.*	– *You are too clingy & touchy-feely.*	– *He didn't feel he had sent her any negative messages.*	– *You aren't quite the person I want you to be.* – *You need to work harder to better yourself.*

STEP 2.

Now compare the negative messages you have given your partner with the negative messages your parents gave you. Are they similar? When you consider what percentage of your five functions were lost to you because they were not supported by your parents, ask yourself what percentage of your partner's functioning you have been responsible for repressing through your own negative messages to him or her.

EXAMPLE:

Andy was saddened to realize that he had attempted to inhibit those parts of Erica that his parents didn't approve of in him. Specifically, he had conveyed to her his opinion that she wasn't as smart as she should be, and that she was too emotionally needy. The net effect of his attitude was that she felt that she had disappointed him as a person. This was exactly the way Andy felt about himself. The only part of Erica that he had totally accepted and approved of was her athleticism. He was upset to realize that this was the part of him that he got most praise for when he was a kid.

Your partner will respond to your attempts to repress by either engaging in conflict with you, or by acquiescing to your wishes. If your partner acquiesces, those parts will be lost to his or her consciousness and become part of his or her lost self. In order for you to stop doing to your partner what was done to you, you must become aware of the messages you are sending. Only then can you support all the functions of your partner.

To recover *your* lost self, ask your partner to help you develop the undeveloped parts of yourself. Study each function in your partner that is missing in you and ask your partner to help you develop that function. You can use your partner as a model to learn how to think, feel, experience all your senses, and move your muscles. You may not develop your function in the same way as your partner, however. For example, your partner may be good at thinking and express it as a philosopher, while you might choose to develop your thinking by becoming a businessperson or a biologist.

When your partner offers help to develop a function, or if you choose to develop it on your own, use your capacity for separate knowing to take in the new information. Then, exercise your capacity for connected knowing by allowing the information to resonate with your feelings and your whole being. Let it be real in your imagination and feelings, and then express it in new behavior. This entire process of discovery, receiving new information, absorbing its significance, thinking of how to change, and making the changes will use all of your faculties. You will develop your ability to receive and to give, and at the same time balance separate knowing and connected knowing into relational knowing.

STEP 3.

The work of recovering your lost self takes places on many fronts. You have to become aware of what has been lost and then start the process of reclamation. As you know from reading the relevant chapters in *Receiving Love,* this involves learning to love in your partner what you find most difficult to love.

In addition, however, there are smaller efforts that can be made to help you begin to transform unconscious losses to conscious attributes. One simple example is to rehearse your new and desired beliefs by converting all of the negative messages about your four functions of self and your core self to positive messages.

For example, convert a "don't . . ." message to your core self to "it's okay to . . ." Convert a "don't move" message to your muscles to "it's okay to move my body." Convert a "don't be sexual" message to your senses to "it's okay to be sexual." Convert a "don't feel" message to "it's okay to feel all my feelings." Convert a "don't think" message to "it's okay to think all my thoughts."

Use the following form to list the negative messages you have received, and *how you are going to convert them to positive messages.*

My negatives messages about *thinking*:

_____

_____

_____

will now become positive messages about *thinking*:

_____

_____

_____

My negative messages about *feeling*:

_____

_____

_____

will now become positive messages about *feeling*:

_____

_____

_____

My negative messages about *sensing*:

_____

_____

_____

will now become positive messages about *sensing*:

_____

_____

_____

My negative messages about *moving*:

_____

_____

_____

will now become positive messages about *moving*:

_____

_____

_____

My negative messages about my *core self*:

_____

_____

_____

will now become positive messages about my *core self*:

_____

_____

_____

EXAMPLE:

Andy wrote down these positive messages. From "There is only one right way, which must be accessed through logic" he wrote this positive statement about thinking: **I am able to develop and use my connected knowing abilities, and I am as capable of thinking things through as anyone.**

From "Feelings are dangerous," he wrote this positive statement about feeling: **It is good for me to acknowledge all my feelings. They make me a more complete person.**

From "Art and beauty are for sissies," he wrote this positive statement about his senses: **It's okay to enjoy music and to create a beautiful home environment.** *His messages about moving were positive, so he reinforced them by writing:* **I want to continue to enjoy working out and rock climbing.**

From "My true self is not acceptable," he wrote this positive statement about his core self: **I am a unique person with important contributions to make just as I am.**

The degree of thoughtfulness and intentionality you bring to this positive conversion really makes a difference. You might ask your partner to say your positive messages to you. Take your time to receive them, think, feel, touch, act, and absorb them into your being. While these are small steps toward becoming whole, every effort you make counts.

BETWEEN-SESSION ASSIGNMENTS

- Choose a different one of your lost parts each week, and take one positive action toward reclaiming it for yourself.
- Have an Imago Dialogue with your partner once a week about the lost self-part you have chosen to reclaim and the action you took to bring it back into yourself. Talk to your partner about how it felt to be engaging in an activity that has been lost to you. Ask your partner to share the same with you.
- Continue to make entries in your Gift Diary Notebook as discussed in Session 1, pages 16–23. Taking a few minutes every day to note the many gifts you receive in your life will help you continue to live in an atmosphere of abundance.

Becoming Whole Again

REVIEW IN *RECEIVING LOVE*

Chapter 4, "Splitting," pages 74–82

Chapter 8, "Separate and Connected Knowing," pages 174–177

Chapter 9, "Practice Relational Knowing," pages 183–185

TIME FRAME

Approximately 50 minutes

SPECIAL CONSIDERATIONS

This last session will help you take the lost parts of yourself and reintegrate them into your awareness and functioning. You will have the opportunity to ask friends and family members to help you in this process. The end result will be a specific plan that identifies your behavior change goals and keeps you focused. This play will be your guide to more personal and relationship satisfaction.

WHAT YOU NEED TO KNOW

All children have natural talents and impulses that express who they are, uniquely as individuals. As a result of praise and support from caretakers, children are encouraged to develop certain aspects of themselves, while disapproval or neglect causes them to *not* develop certain other aspects of themselves. When caretakers criticize talents and impulses, such as sexual curiosity, abstract thinking, or assertiveness, children take the same attitude toward those aspects of themselves as their caretakers did. They see those parts of themselves as bad and dissociate from them in order to survive.

However, ignored or criticized talents and impulses do not disappear. They are simply rejected and pushed out of awareness. They remain in the unconscious and continue to exert significant influence on how the children develop and function.

This means that there is a split within you between the part of you that you know and accept, and the part that is disowned, denied, or lost, either because it is unacknowledged by you or is hidden from you. Your disowned negative traits, denied positive traits, and lost traits lie dormant, locked away from the input that affects the development of the conscious aspects of your personality. These parts do not have the opportunity to express themselves because they are unavailable for communication with the conscious part of yourself or others. These disowned, denied, and lost parts manifest as a sense of emptiness, accompanied by unspecific longings, and are the source of self-hatred and low self-esteem.

In *addition,* when only part of you is available to your conscious self, you don't have access to all of your skills, intuitions, and abilities. Instead of interacting with others through relational knowing, you become imbalanced and overemphasize either separate or connected knowing. If your thinking is blocked, your emotions tend to overshadow rational thinking. If your emotions are blocked, you tend to be overly cognitive, at the expense of your emotions (see Session 3, "Learning How You Know," pages 35–47).

In order to become whole again—to be able to receive, give, and engage in relational knowing—you must become aware of talents and traits you possess that do not currently fit your concept of self. Completing this session of the workbook will allow your partner to become the primary agent through which you recognize and reintegrate denied, disowned, and lost parts of yourself. In effect, your relationship partner becomes your healing partner, as you both work toward greater wholeness. The more whole you become as individuals, the more your relationship becomes a conscious partnership.

Some of the impulses and traits you have blocked can be considered positive. These are called "disowned" traits. Others appear to be negative or undesirable. These are called "denied" traits. For instance, you may not think of yourself as "creative" and "soft" (disowned traits), or "distant" and "critical" (denied traits). Lost traits are those parts of yourself that you have neither disowned nor denied—both acts of decision—but those that you are simply not aware of. All of these unsupported parts together constitute your lost self.

The people who know you well, such as your partner, friends, or family members, may have already observed and reported these traits to you. Since the major characteristic of a disowned or denied trait is its invisibility to you and its visibility to other people in your environment, you may not be able to relate to what people are telling you when they attribute such characteristics to you.

The way you can know whether a positive or negative trait is descriptive of your disowned or denied selves is whether more than one person has reported it to you, and if when they do, you have a strong emotional reaction to what they're saying. These are clear signs that the trait describes some aspect of you that others have seen exhibited in a behavior. Since the trait describes some aspect of yourself, your denial of it amounts to an emotional rejection of that aspect of yourself. The fate of a rejected self-part is to be hated, and that leads to the self-hatred that underlies general low self-esteem.

Another fate of these criticized talents and impulses may be their conversion into disowned or denied traits you develop to compensate for the traits you reject. For instance, a person who has denied sexual curiosity may become a crusader against pornography or a prude. Or, early childhood possessiveness that your caretakers labeled "stingy" may turn into a more positive version you refer to as being "careful with money."

On the other hand, you may project disowned, denied, or lost traits onto others either by adoration (if they are positive) or criticism (if they are negative). For instance, you may worship musical talent in others, while denying yourself an outlet for your own musical impulses. Or, you may criticize others as being elitist or "eggheads" while dumbing down your own intelligence. Most often, people project a rejected trait or undeveloped talent onto those closest to them. Through an invisible process of attraction and self-fulfillment, a particular behavior in your partner gets activated by something in you that attracts the projected trait. Projection relieves you of the trait and at the same time allows you to create a relationship with it. In this way you get to experience an unconscious and *false* sense of wholeness, because you have unconsciously used projection onto another person as a means of completing yourself.

These projections, however, have consequences for your relationship with your partner. You may adore a talent you think your partner has, insist that he or she develop it, and disown it in yourself, or you may ignore it as your caretakers did yours. When we project a rejected self-trait onto our partners, we criticize them for having it, expect our partners to admit they have it, and then try to eradicate it. Our partner, then, becomes the victim of the long ago interaction between our caretakers and us.

This session leads to much self-discovery. Reclaiming your whole self feels right and gets you out of the dead-end trap of envying or condemning other people, particularly your partner, for traits that you yourself have. In addition, you will be able to build new behaviors based on the new information you've learned about yourself.

PART I: Discovering Your Disowned and Denied Self

EXERCISE

What Is There About You That You're Not Seeing?

Time: 25 minutes

OBJECTIVE

• To learn what parts of yourself you have disowned and denied.

To free your partner from paying the emotional price for your childhood wounds, it is important that you know and admit you have traits that are inconsistent with your concept of self. When you've done that, you will be able to relate to your partner as a distinct person, rather than as a mirror of the disowned and denied aspects of yourself.

STEP 1.

To discover disowned and denied aspects of yourself, list the positive adjectives that describe your caretakers, partner, and ex-partners *above* the horizontal line in the circle provided. These are the traits you admire or adore in people of the opposite sex, and those of your own gender.

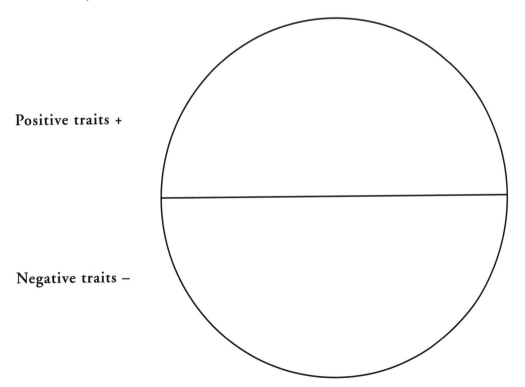

Positive traits +

Negative traits −

List negative adjectives that you assign to your caretakers, partner, and ex-partners *below* the horizontal line. These are the traits you dislike or despise in people of the opposite sex, and those of your own gender.

Now study the circle carefully. The top half of the circle suggests positive traits that you may possess, but disown. The traits listed below the horizontal line suggest negative self-traits that you may possess, but deny. The combination of these disowned positive traits and denied negative traits suggests a description of your rejected self.

EXAMPLE:

Carol completed the steps in the following way:

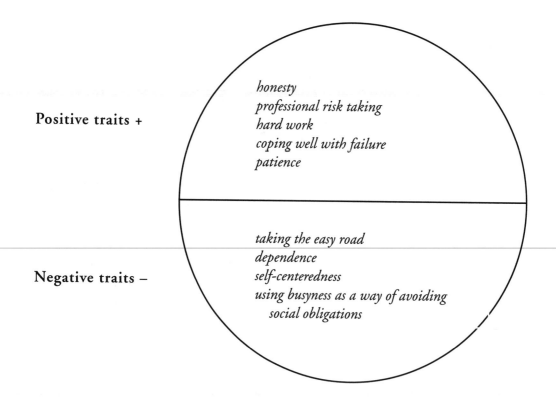

Positive traits +

> *honesty*
> *professional risk taking*
> *hard work*
> *coping well with failure*
> *patience*

Negative traits –

> *taking the easy road*
> *dependence*
> *self-centeredness*
> *using busyness as a way of avoiding*
>   *social obligations*

STEP 2.

If you want to validate this process, ask three to five persons who know you well to make a list of adjectives they think describes you and/or their experience of you. Ask them to hold nothing back and to put a + sign or a − sign beside each trait.

EXAMPLE:

When Carol asked her best friend, her sister, and an old friend from childhood to list the positive and negative adjectives they thought described her, she was able to add to her original lists.

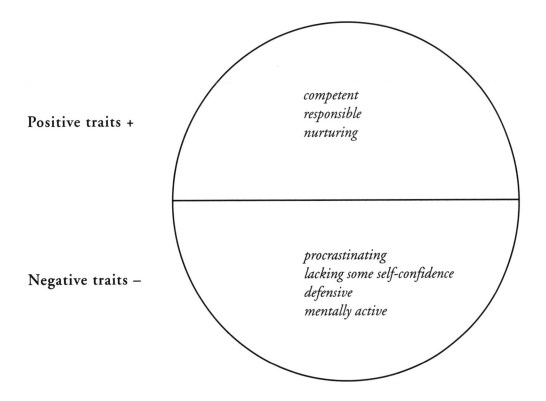

Positive traits +

competent
responsible
nurturing

Negative traits −

procrastinating
lacking some self-confidence
defensive
mentally active

It was hard for Carol to hear what those close to her had to say. Hearing the praise was just as hard as hearing the negatives. But when it was over, she was glad she'd done it. Once these characteristics were named and acknowledged, she knew she could address them directly.

STEP 3.

Next, take all the positive and negative traits from your circle and from all the lists your loved ones compiled for you, and enter them on the chart below. Put positive and negative traits in the appropriate columns. The final chart will be a refined and accurate description of your disowned and denied self-traits.

CHARACTER TRAITS LIST

Column A–Positive Traits	Column B–Negative Traits

STEP 4.

Rank each item on both lists from 1–5, with 1 being the trait you think is most unlike you and 5 being the trait that is most like you.

STEP 5.

Pick five traits from both columns that have the ranking closest to 1 and put them on the chart below according to the categories. The trait *least* descriptive of you is #1, #2 is less descriptive, #3 is somewhat descriptive, #4 is somewhat more descriptive, and #5 is more descriptive. When you finish this step, you will have identified a total of ten traits, five positive and five negative.

SELF-ASSESSMENT OF DISOWNED AND DENIED TRAITS

Ranking	Positive Traits (Column A)	Negative Traits (Column B)
1. Least Descriptive	_____	_____
2. Less Descriptive	_____	_____
3. Somewhat Descriptive	_____	_____
4. Somewhat More Descriptive	_____	_____
5. More Descriptive	_____	_____

CAROL'S SELF-ASSESSMENT OF DISOWNED AND DENIED TRAITS

Ranking	Positive Traits (Column A)	Negative Traits (Column B)
1. Least Descriptive	nurturing	taking the easy road
2. Less Descriptive	patient	lacking some self-confidence
3. Somewhat Descriptive	adventurous	self-centered
4. Somewhat More Descriptive	hardworking	dependent
5. More Descriptive	honest	procrastinating

PART II: Your Personal Growth Plan

Recognizing and honoring your disowned and denied traits is an essential first step in growing beyond your current, self-imposed limitations. This part of the session will guide you in using the information you have just acquired to become a fuller, more authentic individual. In addition, knowing and accepting your whole self allows you to approach relationships with more confidence and self-esteem.

EXERCISE

Integrating Your Disowned and Denied Self

Time: 25 minutes

OBJECTIVES

- To begin to integrate the disowned and denied aspects of yourself into your conscious self-image.

- To turn self-rejection into opportunities for growth.

Follow the step-by-step instructions to achieve a more integrated picture of who you are as an individual, and to learn a more effective way of connecting with your partner.

STEP 1.

Move the five traits in Column A—Positive Traits—in the chart above to the appropriate columns in the chart below.

A Positive Traits	Potential Traits	Behavioral Expression	D

STEP 2.

Then move the traits in Column B—Negative Traits—in the chart above to the appropriate column in the chart below.

B Negative Traits	Potential Traits	Behavioral Expression	D

STEP 3.

The traits in Column A represent positive potential you possess that other people already see, but that you may have denied. You need to claim and integrate these traits into your self-concept. You can do this by changing the name of a positive trait that may feel like too much of a stretch to a potential trait that you want to develop. You can list potential traits in the space provided for all five positive traits, if necessary. Then, design a behavior that expresses the positive or potential trait in interpersonal transactions. The behavior should be positive, concrete, specific, and quantified. Use the space provided and record behavioral expressions for each of the five positive or potential traits. Next, rank the behaviors 1–5 with "1" as most difficult, in Column D.

For instance, if one of the traits is "creative," you can keep that word or choose a similar word, such as "insightful." If you keep "creative" you could express it behaviorally as follows: "I will write and draw in my journal every day for the next month."

STEP 4.

Now change the five traits in Column B to traits that would be positive and desirable. Changing to an opposite trait is okay, if that is the new trait you want to develop.

For instance, if you listed "stingy" as a trait, then you can change it to "prudent" and express it behaviorally as follows: "I will establish a savings plan that will enable me to save steadily over the next 12 months."

A Positive Traits	Potential Traits	Behavioral Expression	D
Nurturing	*Compassionate*	*I will listen better to my partner*	*1*
Patient	*Caring about details*	*I will be alert to small ways I can make my partner feel good*	*2*
Adventurous	*Physically active*	*I will find outdoor activities for us to do together*	*3*
Hardworking	*Reliable*	*I will improve my skills on the job*	*4*
Honest	*Has integrity*	*I will use this quality to continue to improve my relationships*	*5*

B Negative Traits	Potential Traits	Behavioral Expression	D
Taking easy road	*I know how to love myself*	*I will monitor my stress level and give myself a break when I need to*	*1*
Lacking in self-confidence	*I welcome input from others*	*I will learn how to hear what my partner has to say while still holding on to my own ideas and feelings*	*2*
Self-centered	*I am self-aware*	*I will continue with individual counseling with the goal of becoming a better partner*	*3*
Dependent	*I know how to be in partnership*	*I will be aware of ways I can increase my self-ness at the same time I appreciate my partner's self-ness*	*4*
Procrastinating	*Fearless*	*I will use my organizational skills and conscious intention to plunge into work despite my fears*	*5*

Carol referred to her personal growth plan every morning as she ate breakfast. She wanted to reinforce her decision to make changes in her behavior that reflected her determination to turn the disowned and denied parts of herself into positive aspects of her personality. Her growth plan kept her on track and let her feel pleased at the progress she was making. For example, when she had an opportunity to speak in front of a professional organization, she accepted because she remembered that her friends and her sister thought she wasn't as confident in her abilities as they thought she should be.

As you complete this session, you are flexing your capacities for thinking and analyzing. In other words, you are engaging in separate knowing. Actually practicing your personal growth plan requires that you use connected knowing. Being able to participate in both ways of knowing and move comfortably between them increases your capability as a relational knower.

STEP 5.

After you complete Step 4, ask your partner for an Imago Dialogue. The purpose of this dialogue will be to share your growth plans with each other. Choose a time and place that works for both of you. Decide who will be the Sender and who will be the Receiver. Then, follow this process.

- The Sender tells the Receiver about his or her Personal Growth Plan. For example, if Carol were the Sender, she would tell her partner how she intends to use her positive and transformed positive traits to change her behavior, and how this will improve their relationship. She would give examples and add any additional comments that would help clarify her message.
- The Receiver mirrors what the Sender has just said, and asks, *"Did I get that right?"*
- If the Receiver mirrored accurately, the Sender continues by summarizing what he or she has learned by completing her plan and what it means for their relationship.
- The Receiver mirrors and checks to see if the mirror is accurate.
- If the Receiver mirrored accurately, he or she asks if there is more the Sender wants to say.
- If not, then the Receiver proceeds to the steps of validating and empathizing.
- Then switch places, and it is the Sender's turn to receive and the Receiver's turn to send, following the same process as before.

Make a commitment to practice your new behaviors regularly. Sooner than you think, your new behaviors will become habits, and your habits will become an integral part of who you are.

POST-SESSION ASSIGNMENTS

- In an Imago Dialogue, share with your partner at least once a week about which of your desired, new behaviors you have practiced. Tell your partner why you chose this particular aspect of yourself to work on, how you practiced it, and how it felt to experience yourself doing it.
- Invite your partner to share in an Imago Dialogue with you his or her experiences in practicing new behaviors. Communicating about your journey as you progress through this new stage of your life will keep you connected and will ensure that you evolve together.

THE END IS A NEW BEGINNING

You and your partner have done a tremendous amount of work in these twelve sessions. You have learned a lot about yourselves individually and about your relationship. You have had the opportunity to excavate past experiences to see how they continue to influence you. You have uncovered attitudes, patterns of behavior, and capacities you were unaware of. Most important, you have acquired new tools for making use of what you have learned.

A tool is only as effective as your use of it. Find a way to keep practicing what you've learned about creating positive interactions with each other. That means, keep using the Imago Dialogue. Plan at least one formal Imago Dialogue every week and stay aware of the spirit of dialogue in *all* your interactions.

Remember to interject the positive in your lives together. Continue to give each other gifts, practice positive flooding, eliminate criticism, listen well to each other, and tread softly in those places you now know are tender. When either of you overcomes an obstacle or achieves a new level of competence, make a specific plan together to celebrate your accomplishments. Your celebration can be as simple as allowing yourself a dish of your favorite ice cream or watching a movie together, or as sophisticated as taking a vacation.

Know that thousands of couples have been able to transform tired or acrimonious relationships to ones that are alive and exciting. You wanted this kind of relationship enough to undertake this process in the first place. Now, use your capacity for focus and determination to stay with it. Countless blessings will come into your life and your relationship as a result.

APPENDIX

ADDITIONAL FORMS

SESSION 3: ARE YOU A SEPARATE OR CONNECTED KNOWER?

SEPARATE KNOWING

You have an exaggerated reliance on *separate knowing* when you:

_____ 1. Listen to what others are saying with a critical ear.

_____ 2. Examine arguments analytically, looking for flaws in the reasoning, insisting that every point be justified.

_____ 3. Take an adversarial stance toward the ideas of others, even when the ideas seem appealing.

_____ 4. Do not see the other person and what he or she is saying as unique, but see that person as an instance of a category or genre.

_____ 5. Do not enter into the experience of the other person and imagine yourself in that person's place.

_____ 6. Are most comfortable when the other person is responding to you on the basis of the impersonal, cognitive content of your ideas and not on an emotional basis.

Other clues that you are a *separate knower* exist when other people notice that you:

_____ 7. Speak clearly, succinctly, and logically, but with little if any *affect* (visible, nonverbal communication).

_____ 8. Are impatient when other people elaborate their points excessively.

_____ 9. Do not convey warmth or sympathy.

CONNECTED KNOWING

You have exaggerated reliance on *connected* knowing when you:

_____ 1. Listen with an empathic, receptive ear.

_____ 2. Do not demand that other people justify what they are saying.

_____ 3. Wonder to yourself, when you disagree with what's being said, *What in their experience has led them to that point of view?*

_____ 4. Want to understand what is being said instead of testing its validity.

_____ 5. Try to embrace new ideas, looking for what makes sense even in positions that seem initially wrongheaded or abhorrent.

_____ 6. Are willing to enter into stories beyond the bounds of your own experience and attempt to find meaning in narratives that, at first blush, make little sense.

_____ 7. Are not comfortable when people respond to you, not with a sense of shared understanding, but primarily with analyses, solutions, and other impersonal approaches.

Other clues that you are a *connected knower* exist when other people can observe that:

_____ 8. You cannot say what you mean succinctly.

_____ 9. Your partner and others become impatient with your elaborations.

_____10. Your partner and others say that you get overly emotional.

As you consider each of the sentences, if you think you are a separate knower, give yourself a rating of 1–4 on the SK side of the scale. If you think you are a connected knower, give yourself a rating of 1–4 on the CK side of the scale. These numbers represent the degree to which you think you manifest this trait. The number "1" indicates that you think you are strongly one way or the other; the number "4" indicates that you think you are weakly one way or the other. The closer your rating is to the center (number "5"), the closer you are to being a relational knower.

SK	1	2	3	4	5	4	3	2	1	CK

SESSION 5: EXPANDING THE POSITIVE FLOODING

In the chart on the next page, write down those aspects of yourself you would like your partner to flood with praise and appreciation. In the Global Affirmations column include whatever you wished you had heard in your childhood, and whatever you would like to hear from your partner if you had the relationship of your dreams.

Physical Characteristics	Character Traits	Behaviors	Global Affirmations

SESSION 6: EXAMINING YOUR RECEPTIVITY

STEP 1.

Below are 50 questions designed to help you discover what we are calling your "receiving quotient." Answer how often you do what is stated by marking each item with S for "sometimes," O for "often," or N for "never" or "rarely." The number of Ns will measure your "positive receiving quotient." The number of Ss and Os will measure your "negative receiving quotient."

Take your time thinking about each question. Use your capacities for separate and connected knowing as you respond. Evaluate each statement from a factual perspective, and consider each one from a more intuitive, emotional perspective. To get a complete and honest picture of how well you are able to receive and witness receiving, you must call upon your ability to assess yourself from both perspectives.

1.____Do you feel uncomfortable when someone brags about you?

2.____Do you feel critical when someone brags about himself or herself?

3.____Do you feel negative toward someone else who is bragged about by another person?

4.____Do you feel critical when someone lets himself be bragged about?

5.____Do you ever get a gift and feel obligated?

6.____Do you ever get gifts and forget you got them?

7.____Do you ever devalue the gifts others give you?

8.____Do you ever refuse to take gifts?

9.____Do you ever deflect compliments when you get them?

10.____Do you ever ask for something, get it, and find something wrong with it?

11.____Do you ever find yourself mainly remembering only the "bad times"?

12.____Do you ever ask for something, get it, and then forget that you asked for it?

13.____Do you ever ask for something, get it, and then forget that you got it?

14.____Do you ask for the same thing over and over again?

15.____Does it ever seem to you that no one wants you to have what you want?

16.____Do you ever tell stories of not getting what you asked for?

17._____Do you ever say, "I want you to offer it," and when your partner does, say your partner offered it only because you asked for it?

18._____Do you ever feel uncomfortable when another person is getting all the attention?

19._____Do you ever feel like "nothing is good enough"?

20._____Do you ever feel uncomfortable wanting things for yourself?

21._____Do you ever feel uncomfortable with your desires?

22._____Do you say you don't want something and then complain about not getting it?

23._____Do you see everyone else as having what he or she wants?

24._____Do you envy other people having good things you don't have?

25._____Do you ever have trouble accepting others' positive valuations of you—your worth, ability?

26._____Do you ever see someone else receive something you don't feel he or she deserves?

27._____Do you ever feel uncomfortable giving something to yourself?

28._____Do you ever feel critical of someone who whines?

29._____Do you ever feel critical of someone who is needy?

30._____Do you ever feel like a bad person?

31._____Do you ever feel worthless?

32._____Do you ever feel like a failure?

33._____Do you ever feel depressed?

34._____Do you feel chronic anger at others who are fortunate?

35._____Do you ever feel like you put forth a false "good" self and hide your true "bad" self?

36._____Do you ever have trouble imagining why others like and accept praise?

37._____Do you ever feel critical of people who ask for reassurance?

38._____Do you ever feel uncomfortable with people who want nurturing?

39._____Do you feel uncomfortable when other people ask for things from you?

40._____Do you ever feel like you have nothing to give?

41._____Do you ever think that if you take what you ask for you can't ask for anything else?

42._____Do you ever feel that if you get what you want, you can't complain anymore?

43._____Do you get jealous of those who have what they want?

44._____Do you ever feel you have been destined by fate to suffer deprivation?

45._____Do you feel deprived by fate of your blessings?

46._____Do you ever get a compliment and think, *If you knew what I was really like, you would not say that*?

47._____Do you ever feel useless?

48._____Do you ever get gifts and then give them away?

49._____Do you ever feel uncomfortable asking for nurturing?

50._____Do you ever get what you ask for and then feel empty?

STEP 2.

Each item on the list is worth one point for a total of 50 points. To calculate your "positive receiving quotient," count the items marked N. To calculate your "negative receiving quotient," count the total items marked S and O. If your N number is greater than your S and O number, then your "positive receiving quotient" is higher than your "negative receiving quotient." That is, you generally find it easier to accept gifts than to turn them away, and to witness others receiving gifts, rather than ignoring the event. If your S and O number is higher than your N number, then you have a higher "negative receiving quotient" and being receptive to gifts and witnessing others receiving gifts is a major challenge for you.

SESSION 7: EXAMINING HOW GIVING YOU ARE

STEP 1.

Below are 50 questions designed to help you discover what we are calling your "giving quotient." Please answer how often you do what is stated by marking each item with S for "sometimes," O for "often," or N for "never" or "rarely." The number of Ss and Os will measure your "positive giving quotient." The number of Ns will measure your "negative giving quotient."

As was true when assessing your "receiving quotient," allow yourself to consider your answers from both a separate and connected knowing perspective. Consider each statement from the point of view that examines the facts of your behavior, and the emotional point of view that considers your feelings.

1. _____ I feel comfortable bragging about someone.

2. _____ I feel positive when someone brags about himself or herself.

3. _____ I feel positive toward someone else who is bragged about by another person.

4. _____ I give gifts without expecting others to feel obligated.

5. _____ I give gifts and do not remember I gave them.

6. _____ I give gifts to people who value them.

7. _____ I accept people who refuse to take my gifts.

8. _____ I give compliments to others easily.

9. _____ I express love easily and freely.

10. _____ I tend to remember only the good times.

11. _____ When I give a gift, I do not expect to be thanked.

12. _____ I express appreciation for the gifts other people give me.

13. _____ I try to give gifts that other people say they want.

14. _____ I give without telling stories about my giving.

15. _____ I like giving anonymous gifts.

16. _____ I feel comfortable when another person is getting all the attention.

17. _____ I give to needy people.

18. _____ I feel comfortable giving to myself.

19. _____ I have a desire to give.

20. _____ I give without complaining.

21. _____ I like seeing other people have what they want.

22. _____ I share the joy of other people who have good things I don't have.

23. _____ I positively affirm the value of other people—their worth, their ability.

24. _____ I feel full inside when I give.

25. _____ I feel comfortable when other people give things to themselves.

26.____I believe giving expands me.

27.____I feel loving toward people who are needy.

28.____I feel like I am a good person.

29.____I value myself.

30.____I feel like a success.

31.____I feel happy most of the time.

32.____I celebrate the good fortune of other people.

33.____I try to show my best self at all times.

34.____I support others who like and want praise.

35.____I willingly reassure others who need it or ask for it.

36.____I feel comfortable nurturing others.

37.____I feel comfortable when others ask me for something.

38.____I feel like I have a lot to give.

39.____I feel a lot of joy when I give.

40.____I give full attention to people who complain.

41.____I love it when other people get what they want.

42.____I give full attention to people when they are talking to me.

43.____I give praise to God or to fate for my blessings.

44.____I give myself good health care.

45.____I like it when someone lets themselves be bragged about.

46.____I always feel valuable and useful.

47.____I feel blessed to be able to give.

48.____I give gifts to persons whom I don't like.

49.____I am glad to be alive.

50.____I praise God for the gift of life.

STEP 2.

Each item on the list is worth one point for a total of 50 points. To calculate your "positive giving quotient," which is your ability to give, count the total items marked S and O. To calculate your "negative giving quotient," or the difficulty you have with giving, count the items marked N. If your N number is greater than your S and O number, then your "negative giving quotient" is higher than your "positive giving quotient." If your S and O number is higher than your N number, then you have a higher "positive giving quotient."

SESSION 8, PART I: WHAT I GOT FROM MY PARENTS OR OTHER CARETAKERS

STEP 1.

On the chart below, or on a separate sheet of paper, make a list of positive and negative traits that describe your parents or other significant caretakers, as you recall them.

| | MOTHER | | FATHER |
Positive Traits	Negative Traits	Positive Traits	Negative Traits

STEP 2.

Read through the list below and think about which of these attributes was acceptable to want in your family. Which were valued and sanctioned as allowable objects of desire? For simplicity's sake, circle the ones that were acceptable regardless of whether the okay came from your mother, your father, or other caretakers. The adult figures in your life probably had quite different ideas about what was okay and what wasn't, but all we want to do now is get a clearer idea of what messages *you* got in childhood, whatever the source.

In my family it was okay to want: love, sex, play, fun, intelligence, body touch, nurturing, rest, movement, feelings, sleep, education, work, success, happiness, health, food, vacations, spirituality, religious beliefs, touch, laughter, support, warmth, praise, knowledge, your own thoughts, sympathy for others, money, property, recreation, freedom, independence, compliments, negative feelings, hope, orgasms, massages, fear, sadness, anger, grief, joy, peace, equality, pleasure, musical talent, creativity, artistic talent, faith, doubt, desires, athletic talent, competition, trust, fatigue, respect, tolerance, appreciation, gratitude, empathy (add any other words that you wish).

Now, read through the list again and draw a single line through the attributes that it was **not** okay to want in your family.

*In my family it was **not** okay to want:* love, sex, play, fun, intelligence, body touch, nurturing, rest, movement, feelings, sleep, education, work, success, happiness, health, food, vacations, spirituality, religious beliefs, touch, laughter, support, warmth, praise, knowledge, your own thoughts, sympathy for others, money, property, recreation, freedom, independence, compliments, negative feelings, hope, orgasms, massages, fear, sadness, anger, grief, joy, peace, equality, pleasure, musical talent, creativity, artistic talent, faith, doubt, desires, athletic talent, competition, trust, fatigue, respect, tolerance, appreciation, gratitude, empathy (add any other words that you wish).

STEP 3.

Use the chart below to list what was okay to want, and **not** okay to want, in your family.

It was okay to want: It was **not** okay to want:

_____ _____

_____ _____

_____ _____

_____ _____

STEP 4.

Identifying what was okay to want in your family will help you see what was acceptable to receive and to give. Answering the questions below will take some time and thought. There isn't necessarily a linear relationship between wanting, receiving, and giving. For example, in some instances, you might feel that it's okay to give a particular thing, but not okay to receive it yourself.

Refer back to the list you made in Step 3. As you consider each attribute on your positive and negative lists, ask yourself whether it was okay or **not** okay to receive and give each one. Then fill in the following statements about receiving and giving.

In my family, it was okay to expect to receive, or to receive: _____

_____

_____

_____

In my family it was **not** okay to expect to receive, or to receive: _____

_____

_____

_____

In my family it was okay to expect to give, or to give: _____

_____

_____

_____

In my family it was **not** okay to expect to give, or to give: _____

_____

_____

_____

STEP 5.

You have just identified some of the central messages you received from your parents, or other caretakers, about what you could give and what you could receive. Now take this information a step further and write down what consequences were attached to obeying or disobeying these negative and positive messages.

If I obeyed the negative messages, then: _____

_____

_____

_____

If I **disobeyed** the negative messages, then: _____

_____

_____

_____

If I obeyed the positive messages, then: _____

_____

_____

_____

If I **disobeyed** the positive messages, then: _____

_____

_____

_____

STEP 6.

From these general statements, use the following form to write down which messages you obeyed, which you disobeyed, and what the consequences were.

The negative messages I obeyed were _____

_____

_____

_____

and the consequences were _____

_____

_____

_____

The negative messages I **disobeyed** were _____

_____

_____

_____

and the consequences were _____

_____

_____

_____

The positive messages I obeyed were _____

_____

_____

_____

and the consequences were _____

_____

_____

_____

The positive messages I **disobeyed** were _____

_____

_____

_____

and the consequences were _____

_____

_____

_____

STEP 7.

Now, given the messages you obeyed, what decisions did you make about:

Who I am: _____

_____

_____

_____

What I deserve: _____

_____

_____

_____

What I don't deserve: _____

_____

_____

_____

Given who I am, what I deserve, and what I don't deserve, I can expect from life that: _____

_____

_____

_____

These expectations have had an impact on what kind of partner I have chosen and what I can expect from my intimate relationship. From my intimate relationship, I can expect:

_____

_____

_____

STEP 8.

You can get a clearer understanding of how your childhood messages have carried forward into your current life by answering the following questions.

Which messages are you still obeying? _____

_____

_____

_____

What consequences are you still experiencing? _____

_____

_____

_____

STEP 9.

Finally, let's look at which of these early childhood messages are no longer serving you well.

Which early messages do you want to change? _____

_____

_____

_____

Instead of these old messages, what new messages do you want to guide your life?

_____

_____

_____

What will you have to change about yourself to negate the old messages and instill the new ones? _____

_____

_____

_____

SESSION 8, PART II: THE BELIEFS MY PARTNER BROUGHT TO OUR RELATIONSHIP

STEP 1.

Your caretakers aren't the only source of messages about which attitudes and beliefs toward giving and receiving are acceptable and which aren't. You have probably been influenced by former partners, teachers, coaches, friends, bosses, and coworkers, just to name a few. Of these, though, your current partner is probably the most influential. Since this exercise asks you for your opinion about which messages he or she sends you, it is entirely subjective. It could be that in some instances, *you think* your partner holds a particular belief, but you are wrong. Your own projection has colored your assessment. Nevertheless, based on our years of experience working with couples, we predict that your responses will be accurate most of the time.

Using the same list of attributes we used in Part I, circle the ones that are okay to want according to your partner.

My partner has let me know it's okay to want: love, sex, play, fun, intelligence, body touch, nurturing, rest, movement, feelings, sleep, education, work, success, happiness, health, food, vacations, spirituality, religious beliefs, laughter, support, warmth, praise, knowledge, your own thoughts, sympathy for others, money, property, recreation, freedom, independence, compliments, negative feelings, hope, orgasms, massages, fear, sadness, anger, grief, joy, peace, equality, pleasure, musical talent, creativity, artistic talent, faith, doubt, desires, athletic talent, competition, trust, belief, fatigue, respect, tolerance, appreciation, gratitude, empathy (add any other words that you wish).

Now, review the list again and draw a single line through those things that are **not** okay to want according to your partner.

*My partner has let me know it's **not** okay to want:* love, sex, play, fun, intelligence, body touch, nurturing, rest, movement, feelings, sleep, education, work, success, happiness, health, food, vacations, spirituality, religious beliefs, laughter, support, warmth, praise, knowledge, your own thoughts, sympathy for others, money, property, recreation, freedom, independence, compliments, negative feelings, hope, orgasms, massages, fear, sadness, anger, grief, joy, peace, equality, pleasure, musical talent, creativity, artistic talent, faith, doubt, desires, athletic talent, competition, trust, belief, fatigue, respect, tolerance, appreciation, gratitude, empathy (add any other words that you wish).

STEP 2.
Use the chart below to list what your partner thinks is okay to want and **not** okay to want.

It is okay to want:

_____

_____

_____

_____

It is **not** okay to want:

_____

_____

_____

_____

STEP 3.
Based upon the lists you compiled in Step 2, complete the sentences below with messages *you think* your partner received from his or her caretakers.

My partner feels it's okay to expect to receive, or to receive: _____

_____

_____

_____

My partner feels it's **not** okay to expect to receive, or to receive: _____

_____

_____

_____

My partner feels it's okay to expect to give, or to give: _____

_____

_____

_____

My partner feels it's **not** okay to expect to give, or to give: _____

_____

_____

_____

STEP 4.

Review the lists you compiled in Step 2 again, and this time, complete the sentences with messages *your partner sends to you.*

In my relationship with my partner, it's okay for me to expect to receive, or to receive:

_____

_____

_____

In my relationship with my partner, it's **not** okay for me to expect to receive, or to receive:

_____

_____

_____

In my relationship with my partner, it's okay for me to expect to give, or to give:

_____

_____

_____

In my relationship with my partner, it's **not** okay for me to expect to give, or to give:

_____

_____

_____

These messages indicate what prohibitions and permissions around receiving and giving exist in your relationship.

SESSION 8, PART III: DECIDING HOW I WANT TO GIVE AND RECEIVE NOW

Write down the messages you wish you had heard from your mother, father, or other significant caretakers; the messages you want to hear from your partner; and the new permissions you will give to yourself regarding giving and receiving.

I wish I had heard these messages about giving and receiving from my mother:

_____

_____

_____

_____

I wish I had heard these messages about giving and receiving from my father:

_____

_____

_____

_____

I want to hear these messages about giving and receiving from my partner:

_____

_____

_____

I now give myself permission to give and receive in these new ways:

_____

_____

_____

_____

SESSION 9: CONCRETE PLAN FOR YOUR RELATIONSHIP GROWTH CHALLENGE

My Relationship Growth Challenge Goal is: _____

_____

_____

_____

Three specific actions I will take to achieve this goal are:

1. I will _____

_____

_____

_____

Indicate time by when you will do this, or how often: _____

_____

_____

_____

2. I will _____

_____

_____

_____

Indicate time by when you will do this, or how often: _____

_____

_____

_____

3. I will _____

_____

_____

_____

Indicate time by when you will do this, or how often: _____

_____

_____

_____

SESSION 10: BEHAVIOR GOALS FOR YOUR DEFENSES

From now on, when I am feeling (enter an example of a negative feeling from Step 1).

_____

_____

_____

_____

I will pause and ask myself (whether my feeling is really a defense).

_____

_____

_____

_____

_____

I will try to be honest and accepting of myself and acknowledge when (refer back to the list of positive statements in Step 3).

_____

_____

_____

_____

_____

Instead of what I have done in the past, which is to be defensive and (refer back to the list of the six defenses in Step 1), I will (behavior goal)

_____

_____

_____

_____

_____

SESSION 11: MESSAGES I GOT FROM MY CARETAKERS ABOUT ASPECTS OF MY SELF

Thinking	Feeling	Sensing	Moving	Core Self

Use the chart on the previous page to record the messages you received from your caretakers. Identify the positive messages with a + sign and the negative messages with a − sign. Count the total number of positive messages you received about each function and the total number of negative messages you received about each one.

SESSION 11: MY LOST SELF FUNCTIONS

On the diagram, record the number of negative and positive messages you received from your caretakers for each function. Study your negative messages for each function and black out your estimate of the percentage of that function you feel was repressed in your childhood.

    The sections of the circle that you black out as repressed functions constitute your "lost self." These functions were rejected by your caretakers and thus by you. The remaining white space reflects the percent of that function that was not repressed.

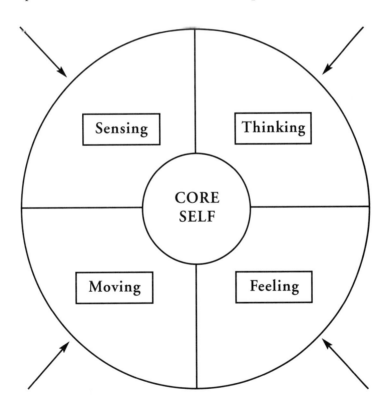

SESSION 11: WHAT MESSAGES DO I SEND TO MY PARTNER?

Think about the statements you make to your partner about his or her freedom to think, to feel feelings, to experience the five senses, to move, and to be his or her core self. Fill out the chart below by recording both the positive and negative messages you've given to your partner.

Thinking	Feeling	Sensing	Moving	Core Self

SESSION 12: DISCOVERING YOUR DISOWNED AND DENIED SELF

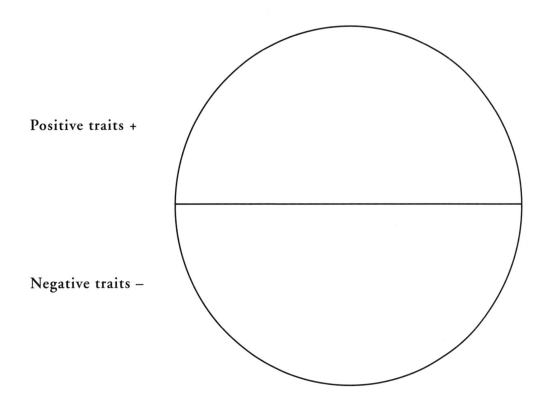

Positive traits +

Negative traits −

STEP 1.

To discover the disowned and denied aspects of yourself, list the positive adjectives that describe your caretakers, partner, and ex-partners *above* the horizontal line. These are the traits you admire or adore in people of the opposite sex, and those of your own gender.

List negative adjectives that you assign to your caretakers, partner, and ex-partners *below* the horizontal line. These are the traits you dislike or despise in people of the opposite sex, and those of your own gender.

Now study the circle carefully. The top half of the circle suggests positive traits that you may possess, but disown. The traits listed below the horizontal line suggest negative self-traits that you may possess, but deny. The combination of these disowned positive traits and denied negative traits suggests a description of your rejected self.

STEP 2.

If you want to validate this process, ask three to five persons who know you well to make a list of adjectives they think describe you and/or their experience of you. Ask them to hold nothing back and to put a + sign or a – sign beside each trait.

CHARACTER TRAITS LIST

Column A–Positive Traits	Column B–Negative Traits

STEP 3.

Rank each item on both lists from 1–5, with 1 being the trait you think is most unlike you and 5 being the trait that is most like you.

STEP 4.

Pick five traits from both columns that have the ranking closest to 1 and put them on the chart below according to the categories. The trait *least* descriptive of you is #1, #2 is less descriptive, #3 is somewhat descriptive, #4 is somewhat more descriptive, and #5 is more descriptive. When you finish this step, you will have identified a total of ten traits, five positive and five negative.

SELF-ASSESSMENT OF DISOWNED AND DENIED TRAITS

Ranking	Positive Traits (Column A)	Negative Traits (Column B)
1. Least Descriptive	_____	_____
2. Less Descriptive	_____	_____
3. Somewhat Descriptive	_____	_____
4. Somewhat More Descriptive	_____	_____
5. More Descriptive	_____	_____

SESSION 12: INTEGRATING YOUR DISOWNED AND DENIED SELF

Follow the step-by-step instructions to achieve a more integrated picture of who you are as an individual, and to help you approach relationships with more confidence and self-esteem.

STEP 1.
Move the five traits in Column A—Positive Traits—in the chart above to the appropriate columns in the chart below.

A Positive Traits	Potential Traits	Behavioral Expression	D

STEP 2.

Then move the traits in Column B—Negative Traits—in the chart above to the appropriate column in the chart below.

B Negative Traits	Potential Traits	Behavioral Expression	D

STEP 3.

The traits in Column A represent positive potential you possess that other people already see, but that you may have denied. You need to claim and integrate these traits into your self-concept. You can do this by changing the name of a positive trait that may feel like too much of a stretch to a potential trait that you want to develop. You can list potential traits in the space provided for all five positive traits, if necessary. Then, design a behavior that expresses the positive or potential trait in interpersonal transactions. The behavior should be positive, concrete, specific, and quantified. Use the space provided and record behavioral expressions for each of the five positive or potential traits. Next, rank the behaviors 1–5, with "1" as most difficult, in Column D.

STEP 4.

Now change the five traits in Column B to traits that would be positive and desirable. Changing to an opposite trait is okay, if that is the new trait you want to develop.

Congratulations! You have now completed the workbook. You have learned how early life experiences have shaped your ability to give and receive gifts, and how you and your partner can keep the channels of giving and receiving open between you. Please treat this workbook as a living resource that you can call on again as you keep your commitment to create a conscious relationship that is happy and fulfilling.

Acknowledgments

We want to thank the many couples whose lives and work are reflected in these pages. Were it not for their vulnerability and courage, this book would never have been conceived, much less written. These include couples who shared their lives in therapy and those who contributed their insights on the healing process in response to our research inquiry and telephone-bridge conversations.

We also want to thank the many Imago Relationship therapists who contributed their experience of working with couples, contributed their wisdom, and helped conduct the research that led to our conclusions.

Although there are many individuals who helped make it possible for us to write this book, we want to give special thanks to Sanam Hoon, our assistant. We thank her for her tireless and splendid management of the couples' research project, and for collating all the interviews into useful information.

About Imago Relationship Therapy

Imago Relationship Therapy is a process that helps couples use their relationship for healing and growth. Its goal is to help intimate partners understand that the unconscious purpose of committed couplehood is to finish childhood and shows them how to transform inevitable conflict into connection, thereby creating the relationship of their dreams. The Imago process is taught by over 2,000 therapists in more than twenty countries and is practiced by millions of couples worldwide.

If you are a couple that wants to consult an Imago therapist;

If you and your partner are interested in belonging to an international couples organization called Imago Couple International;

If you are a clinical professional and want certified training in Imago Relationship Therapy;

If you would like training as an Imago educator;

If you would like to teach the Imago Process for Churches: Couplehood as a Spiritual Path;

If you would like information on couples and singles workshops, seminars, and other books, audio and video tapes;

Please go to www.imagorelationships.org, or call 1-800-729-1121.

About the Authors

Harville Hendrix, Ph.D., in partnership with his wife, Helen LaKelly Hunt, Ph.D., created Imago Relationship Therapy. They are co-founders, with other Imago therapists, of Imago Relationships International, an international non-profit organization that offers training, support, and promotion of the work of 2,000 Imago therapists in twenty-one countries. Both lecture and offer workshops on intimate relationships internationally and have together authored six books. Harville wrote *Getting the Love You Want: A Guide for Couples* and *Keeping the Love You Find: A Personal Guide*, both bestsellers, and is the co-author, with Helen of *Giving the Love that Heals: A Guide for Parents*, also a bestseller, and three meditation books: *The Couple Companion: Meditations and Exercises for Getting the Love You Want*, *The Personal Companion: Meditations and Exercises for Keeping the Love You Find*, and *The Parenting Companion: Meditations and Exercises for Giving the Love that Heals*. Their books are published in over fifty-seven languages. Harville has appeared on many national television shows (thirteen times on the Oprah Winfrey show, winning for her the "most socially redemptive" award for daytime talk shows) and radio shows, and has been written up in numerous newspapers and magazines internationally. In addition to her partnership with Harville, Helen is an author in her own right with a book called *Faith and Feminism* that will be published in 2004. For he distinguished contribution to the women's movement, she has received the Gloria Steinem Award and been inducted into the Women's Hall of Fame. They live in New Mexico and New Jersey and have six children.